THE MONASTERY
OF THE HEART

THE MONASTERY
OF THE HEART

An Invitation to a Meaningful Life

JOAN CHITTISTER

BlueBridge

Published by
BlueBridge
An imprint of
United Tribes Media Inc.
Katonah, New York
www.bluebridgebooks.com

Originally published in hardcover in 2011 (ISBN 9781933346342).
First published in paperback in 2012 (ISBN 9781933346571).

Library of Congress Control Number: 2011006263

Cover design by Angel Guerra
Cover image by Purestock / Getty Images
Text design by Cynthia Dunne

Printed in the United States of America
10 9 8 7 6 5 4 3 2 1

Contents

OUR SERVICE

OUR PROMISE

OUR SPIRITUAL GROWTH

Introduction

To the Many Seekers,

After more than fifty years of life in a monastery, I have begun to sift and sort the effects of it all, asking myself, what—if anything—of monastic life is worth passing on to others in this day and age? What of this life has any impact or import to populations other than monastic communities themselves—and how can those outside traditional monasteries, too, join throngs of monastics over the centuries who have found this life both enriching and enlightening?

This book is, then, a kind of guide and invitation for those seekers who stand in the midst of a seething, simmering world of spiritual as well as secular options, overwhelmed by choices, and looking for the rhythm of a better life. It suggests a model upon which to build—or rebuild—their own lives. It offers a template to guide them through the maze of empty promises, seductive dead ends, and useless panaceas the modern world, a spiritless culture, has to offer.

The search for God is an eternal one. It plagues every generation. It stalks every soul. It is the insistent, eternal cry for meaning, for answers to the questions, Why? And what? And for what purpose? It is the unending awareness that I am not alone in the universe, despite the fact that I do not know where I have come from or to what I'm going. It is the soulful pursuit launched to understand the Beginning of Life and to find the answer to its End. The search for God is the attempt to complete the incomplete in us. And it never stops eating away at the innards of our soul.

Every age, every path, has answered the questions of the spiritual dimensions of life in ways peculiar to itself, in language and symbols and lifestyles it could understand. For some, in the past, the search to unite with the One, with the Energy, with the Life of life, took the form of desert asceticism. For others, it lay in community and communal worship. For many, it was an attempt to withdraw from the business of this world in order to be better attuned to the next.

But for one man, for Benedict of Nursia, the spiritual life lay in simply living *this* life, our *daily* life, well. All of it. Every simple, single action of it. History attests to the proof of the power of such a life lived to turn the ordinary into an experience of the extraordinary union with the God of the Universe—here and now. Benedictine spirituality, the ongoing legacy of this sixth-century founder of cenobitic monasticism in the West, to our own times, is proof of its enduring value.

This spirituality based on the Rule of Benedict, a communal lifestyle, is over 1,500 years old. It developed at a time when Europe lay in political, economic, communal, and social disarray. And it exists to this day—around the world. Anything that survives the ages with new vitality in every age is surely worthy of serious spiritual examination in our own.

Most significant, perhaps, is that instead of setting out to reform the decadence of sixth-century Italy, Benedict of Nursia simply ignored the cheap and chaotic superficiality of it all to live according to different standards, to walk a different path, to live the life everyone else lived—but differently. Through the ages, thousands of others have done the same. As a result, Benedictinism has evolved from age to age, until many different forms of its past impulses exist yet—but all of them as carriers of the original impulse.

Today, in this time of cataclysmic social upheavals, of global transitions, of technological breakthroughs of unimagined proportions, we must do the same. Old patterns are breaking down; individuals, families, and small groups everywhere—in intentional communities and home worship, in parishes and prayer groups, through committed lifestyles and private disciplines—are seeking to shape new ways of living for themselves in the shell of the old.

This small guide—following the ancient Rule of Benedict that is still the basic worldview and organizational pattern for life in Benedictine monasteries everywhere—is meant to be a new way to live a meaningful spiritual life in the center of the world today, rather than withdraw from it. It does not abandon traditional Benedictine spirituality in favor of some new or exotic spiritual practice. On the contrary, it is anchored in the Rule, rooted in its values. It is an apple falling off an ancient tree, a cutting meant to grow steeped in its history, fresh in its form.

May the women and men, the families, the intentional communities who seek to create within themselves a Monastery of the Heart, find there the God who is forever seeking them.

OUR SEARCH

1

A Gentle Invitation

*"Listen carefully to my instructions . . . With the good gifts which
are in us, we must obey God."*

To live the God-life,
Benedictine spirituality asserts
as its foundation
that we must immerse ourselves
in the Word of God
as model and guide,
as vision and measure,
of the good and happy life.

To seek God
in a Monastery of the Heart, then,
we must, first of all,
read the scriptures
intensely.

It is in the scriptures
that the eternal vitality
of Benedictine spirituality lies.

It is through immersion
in the Word of God
that the search for meaning
erupts into a life lived in union
with the God
whose presence we seek.

It is through the scriptures
that we follow the Israelites—
chosen as they were,
and yet often as inconstant
as they were—
and see at work in ourselves
all that God saw in them:
the worship of our private little idols
of money and power and status
that lure us away
from the real treasures of life.

We must, at the same time,
come to trust that we carry within us
the same signs of goodness
and faith and desire for life
that took Israel
through the desert of despair

to the Promised Land—
and the opportunity to live
a life dedicated to the will of God.

We must come to see in them
God's continuing patience and love for us,
so that no amount of weakness
in ourselves
can ever discourage us
from continuing
on the Way.
As monastics of the heart we must
read the scriptures day in and day out,
till they ring in our ears,
and fill our hearts,
and become the very breath
we breathe.

We must follow Jesus
from Galilee to Jerusalem,
contending with the system,
healing the people,
doing good,
excluding no one,
being a voice for the voiceless,
calling us all
to follow him to the rising
of the God-life in ourselves.

———

We must put ourselves
under the impulse of the Spirit
and in the hands of the God
who wills us well.

We must give ourselves to the task
of bringing about God's peaceable kingdom,
wherever we are,
in whatever we do.

We must "obey God," the Rule of Benedict says,
"with the good gifts which are in us"—
with all the good, all the love,
all the talent, all the wisdom,
all the care, all the concentration,
all the abandon of soul
that is in us.
We must obey the voices of life
that are being drowned out
around us
but are, nevertheless,
heard by God always.
These are the voices that
call to us to obey
the needs of the world,
the cry of the poor.

They call us to the consciousness
of the power of God's care for us,

and the commitment to make that presence palpable
in the world around us.

There is no one in need
within earshot of our hearts
whom we may ignore—
because in each of them
is the living plea
that we do the will of God.

It is by helping those
who cannot help themselves
that we do our part
in the co-creation of the world.

"Let us ask with the prophet," the Rule says,
"'Who will dwell in your tent, O God;
who will find rest upon your holy mountain?'"

"Then, let us listen well," the Rule goes on,
"to what God says in reply,
for we are shown the way
to God's tent.
'Those who walk without blemish
and are just in all dealings;
who speak truth from the heart
and have not practiced deceit;
who have not wronged another in any way.'"

———

The Benedictine heart echoes
this cry for universal awareness.
The very first word of this ancient Rule,
"Listen,"
is God's constant call,
first to Israel,
daily to us.

It is a gentle, tender invitation,
this call to create within ourselves
a Monastery of the Heart.

It is the call to go down deep
into the self
in order to find there
the God
who urges us
to come out of ourselves
to do the work of God,
to live in union with God
in the world around us.
It is not punitive, this call.
It is not demanding,
not harsh and unforgiving.

It is, instead, the daily guarantee
that, if we will only begin the journey
and stay the road—
listening to the voice of God

and responding to it
with all our gifts and goodness—
we will find that God stands waiting
to sustain us,
and support us,
and fulfill us
at every turn.

God is calling us lovingly always,
if we will only stop the noise within us
long enough to hear.

Benedictine spirituality, then,
is a continuing call to take one more step
on the way back to the God
from whom we have come,
to turn consciously now and here
toward the God
to whom our entire lives
are geared.

The Prologue to Benedict's Rule
demands of us
that we "Listen."

Listen to everything.
Because everything in life is important.
Listen with the heart:
with feeling for the other,

with feeling for the Word,
with feeling for the God
who feels for us.

Listen to the Word of God,
the Rule says,
"and faithfully put it into practice."

Most of all,
know that to seek God
is to find God.

In a Monastery of the Heart—
in the riches of the tradition it offers
and the treasures to which it leads,
and in company with others who are seeking, too—
find a loving spiritual guide
to encourage your journey,
to refresh your faith
when life is dry and dark,
when the days are long and draining,
when you are inclined to forget
that God is with us
for the taking.
Most of all, every day
start over again.

Remember that
life is for coming to see,

one day at a time,
what life and God
are really all about.

Life grows us more and more—
but only if we wrestle daily
with its ever-daily meaning for us.

God is calling us to more
than now—
and God is waiting
to bring us to it.

"Listen," the Rule says.
"If you hear God's voice today,
do not harden your hearts."

2

A Seeker's Path

"Your way of acting should be different from the world's way."

The search for God
is a very intimate enterprise.
It is at the core
of every longing in the human heart.
It is the search for ultimate love,
for total belonging,
for the meaningful life.

It is our attempt
to live life and find it worthwhile,
to come to see the presence of God
under all the phantoms and shadows—
beyond all the illusions of life—
and find it enough.

But the search depends,
at least in part,

on the complex of energies within us
that we bring to the challenges
of this seeking.

We do not all hear the same tones
at the same volume,
or see the same visions
in the same colors,
or seek the same goods of life
in the same way.

The search for God depends, then,
on choosing the spiritual path
most suited to our own spiritual
temper and character.

For some seekers,
it is in withdrawal from society
or by immersion in nature
that God is most present.

For others, the face of God
shows most clearly
in the face of the poor,
or is felt most keenly
through the support of those
with whom they share
a common spiritual regimen.

———

For many, it is a bit of both,
a balance of community,
contemplation,
and commitment
to the people of God.
It is the search to belong
to a group of fellow travelers
who will hold us up
when we fall,
and urge us on to greater heights
when we are afraid to strain for more.

These are the seekers who are looking for others
who seek what they seek,
who care about what they care about,
and who set out with them
to make life richer
and the world better
than they know they could ever do alone.

But whatever the nature
of a seeker's lifestyle,
the search for God
depends, as well,
on the spiritual maturity it takes
to move from one level
of spiritual insight to another—
rather than cling to the spiritual satisfaction
that comes with earlier,

less demanding, practices.
The search for God depends on the desire
to grow to full stature as a spiritual adult,
to come to know the God
who is as present in darkness
as in light.

It depends on the willingness
to let God lead us
through the deserts of a lifetime,
along routes we would not go,
into the Promised Land of our own lives.

Most of all, the search for God
depends on fidelity
to the demands of the search itself.
It is the constancy of commitment
which we bring to the spiritual path
that prepares us
to recognize and receive
the fullness of it.

There is, as a result,
more than one way
to go about the journey
to God.

We may seek God alone,
in the silence of our own hearts,

where our attention is centered
in a keen and conscious way
on developing an ear
for the leavening penetration
in our lives
by the mind and Word of God.

This is an extremely private
and individual spirituality
that emphasizes personal prayer
and contemplation
of the presence of God in life.

But it is not the only way to God
and, in fact, not the most common way.

Another kind of journey to God
leads us to seek God with others
in a covenantal common life,
where by the physical joining of our lives together
we become a daily witness
to create in the world
a community of strangers
bound together by the will of God.

In our time, in a society
that is both mobile
and connected
at the same time,

there is still another
possible way to make the journey to God—
and that is
in a Monastery of the Heart.

Here we choose to seek God
in step with others,
even though not always in common with others—
each of us on an apparently separate path
and yet all of us in veritable community
with one another on the way—
as lifelines,
as mentors,
as guides,
as models,
as brothers and sisters in whose loving company
we choose to make our common journey to God.

The Rule of Benedict recognizes
the major differences among seekers' paths
and alerts us as well to the subtle distinctions
among them,
so that we can begin our own spiritual journey
aware of the complex character of each separate lifestyle,
and prepared to bring our selves to the way best suited
to the enterprise for us.

Going the road alone, for instance—
developing a solitary spiritual discipline—

is a rare but well-worn tradition
of spiritual figures both known and unknown.

Those who go this road to God,
Benedict tells us,
have come to a point in the spiritual life where,
already well-formed in a proven and established
monastic tradition,
they move beyond the structures which maintain it
in order to go deeply
into the struggle with the self—
both physically and mentally—
that comes with solitude.

These seekers, Benedict says,
"Have passed beyond the first fervor of monastic life . . .
They have built up their strength
and go to the single combat of the desert.
Self-reliant now,
they are ready with God's help
to grapple single-handed . . ."

Theirs is the path that strips away
the common supports of life—
the companionship of a partner,
the counsel of others,
the strength of a community,
the traditions of the group—
and throws them on the designs of the Spirit

and deep, deep concentration
on God
alone.

These seekers
feel the impulse of the God within.
They give their lives
to the God who beckons them inward,
sure that the One who calls them
to such a life
will also guide them through it—
alone but not lonely.

The major concern with this lifestyle
is the human tendency to turn in
on ourselves
and to forget our obligation
to build up the entire
human community.
"Whose feet," St. Basil asks,
"will the hermit wash?"

In its stead, Benedict says simply,
are those who
live immersed in a community,
accountable to its standards,
cemented in its values,
and responsible for making
the human community

ever more human,
always more of a community.

In whichever of the lifestyles we find ourselves—
the spiritually solitary of any stage of life,
the intentional living groups of every size,
the networks of similarly committed individuals
whose community life
is stable but not necessarily daily—
we are on tried and true pathways to God.

We are all seekers of the God
who is here
but invisible to the blind eye;
who calls to us
but is unheard by those who do not listen;
who touches our lives wherever we are,
but is unfelt
by those whose hearts
are closed to the presence of God—
who is everywhere,
in everyone,
at all times.

When we seek
to wed all three lifestyles in our own time—
solitary,
intentional,
and communal—

we seek to be
in a Monastery of the Heart.

Then our Rule is this one.
Our spiritual guide is the Word of God.
Our formative community
is with those of one heart with whom
we join on this way
in a Monastery of the Heart—
to find the God who emerges
with inexorable fidelity
in human form.

3

A Single Vision

"Perform the Opus Dei where you are . . .
Those on a journey are not to omit the prescribed hours but to
observe them as best they can."

The Benedictine Rule
is based on the notion
that community life
is the preeminent form
of the spiritual journey,
because it provides for
immersion in communal worship,
private contemplation,
shared wisdom,
common ownership,
and mutual service.

But community life,
life in concert

with like-minded people,
and cloistered life—
life lived with a group
that is independent
of the world around it—
are not necessarily the same thing.

There is no doubt
that the Rule is intent on creating
a community of heart,
a oneness of mind and soul,
a commonness of vision and intent
among the brothers and sisters
that binds them in the common endeavor
of commitment to an intense form
of the spiritual life.

But the Rule
does not necessarily
require community of place—
the geographical confinement
of all the members of one community
to one location.

If and when distance made
common sharing,
common worship,
the common life—
with all the daily human contact and support

such a phrase implies—
impossible,
large monasteries,
whose ministries and members
were far-flung,
have for centuries routinely organized the community
into smaller units of a single system—
such as granges and missions—
for the sake of the intimacy and bonding
that a sense of
real human community demands.

At base,
the Rule asks two major things of us:

First, we are to be constant
at prayer.
We are to perform the work of God—
our commitment to the psalms and scripture—
faithfully,
wherever we are.

In the fields at the hour of prayer,
monastics were to
"kneel out of reverence for God"
rather than return to the monastery
to pray with the entire community.
Clearly, it is prayer itself that is the bond.

———

We are to make prayer
be the bond and constant source
of inspiration and purpose and glue
that holds us together,
the touchstone of everything
that has meaning to us.

We are to pray by ourselves,
if necessary, "as best we can,"
but in the way
the community, as community, is praying,
so that our hearts and minds
stay in the place
where our bodies cannot now be.

Second, we are to live a single vision of life
together, even when apart.
We are to live
Benedictine spirituality
wherever we are,
whatever we are doing.

We are to care for those
who commit themselves with us
to create this new world within a world.

We are to go the way together
in heart and mind and soul.

———

We are to be there for the other
as signs of the coming Reign of God.

We are not to take on
the customs and the conversations,
the values and the interests
of a society
whose heart is in another place
than the one
we nourish in our vision.
We are not to make "away"
our home.

To be "in the world
but not of it"
has always demanded
an uneasy truce
between the monastery
and the society in which it blooms.

But for the Benedictine heart,
to which all things are sacred,
the very act of making
the crooked way straight
and the desert blossom
is itself a trust,
one more reminder of
the sacrament of ordinary life
lived extraordinarily well.

For a monastic to be
anywhere in the world
is meant to be simply another way
of being present
to what and why
we say we are.

Wherever we are,
we are rooted in
the spirituality of the Rule.

A Monastery of the Heart
is our means now
of taking what we have
to where it is needed,
beyond the geography
of a monastery itself.

The function of Benedictine life,
with its community commitment,
is *not* to hide from the world.

It is to make community
for others around it,
to enable others
to also draw from its well.

We join hands with those

who, like us,
are committed to stay this path
until it brings us—
wiser and more seasoned
than when we began—
all the way to God,
all the way home.

The bearer of the monastic heart,
either alone or with an intentional group,
must radiate
what is within
to a wider world
and respond to it.

Those who commit themselves
to live by monastic values
in a Monastery of the Heart
must be bridges to a world without them,
must be models and signs
of another way to live.
They must find their strength
and their purpose
by holding hands with those
who join them on this way,
so that no one can lose contact—
not with the Benedictine tradition
that has spawned them,
not with the society

in which they are embedded,
not with one another—
however far off
the rest of the circle of seekers
may seem.

To the monastic of the heart,
community is not as simple
as geographic location alone,
however important, or good, or growthful
the physical relationship among members
is meant to be.

More than that, community requires
meaningful contact,
a common vision,
and the beating of a cosmic heart
big enough to embrace all of life—
as did Benedict himself
when "he saw the whole world
in a single ray of light."

OUR INTERIOR LIFE

4

Prayer

*"[Let us] lay our petitions before the God of all
with the utmost humility and sincere devotion."*

Benedictine spirituality is rooted
in the timelessness
of scripture.

It is the story of God's way
with the world.

The song of the psalmist,
the cry of the prophet,
the call of Jesus,
the wail of the human heart
for its eternal home,
all resound through the centuries
to beckon us
beyond the emptiness

of momentary desires
to the eternal fullness that is God.

But Benedictine spirituality
is *not* about the past.

Benedictine prayer,
the heartbeat of Benedictine spirituality,
is always about
the presence of God in time—
this time, our time, my time.

Benedictine prayer is not mindless repetition
of endless formulas.
It is about the immersion in the mind of God
that living the God-life requires,
if we are to be faithful to it
all our living days.

Prayer restores the soul
that is dry and dulled
by years of trying
to create a world
that never completely comes.

It heals the wounds of the day
and reminds us who we want to be
at the deepest, truest part of us.

———

Prayer lightens the load.
It gives fresh direction and new energy.
It fixes the eye of the soul
on the real ends of life,
when the real goals of real time
seem unattainable.

It feeds the streams
of silence and sacred reading,
public and private prayer,
that are the pulse
of Benedictine life.

"God regards our purity of heart
and tears of compunction,"
the Rule counsels us,
"not our many words."

Clearly, it is not
the sum of prayers we pray
that counts.
It is the way our prayer life changes
our own hearts and lives—
the way it makes us more centered in God,
the way it makes us more aware of our own limitations—
that determines its quality.

"Prayer should therefore
be short and pure,"

the Rule concludes,
so that it can be an impetus to private prayer,
a basis for personal conversion of heart.

Benedictine prayer is steeped
in the psalms—
the cry of the poor throughout time.

It immerses us in the fullness of the scriptures
and their history of salvation.

It fills us with the Gospel accounts
of the life and message of Jesus.

As regular as the movement of the clock,
Benedictine prayer becomes for us
the pulse of the day,
the rhythm of a life that might otherwise
be caught in the drumbeat
of ambition or profit or self-centeredness.

It is the sustaining force
of a Monastery of the Heart
in a demanding world.

When we might forget
the reasons for which we exist,
the psalms ply us with a universal memory
of the universally poor and oppressed.

If we lose sight in the heat of the day
of the call to co-creation,
Benedictine prayer fixes us on the life of Jesus,
who went from place to place
doing good, healing the sick, raising the dead,
teaching women as well as men,
and contending
with the forces of oppression everywhere.

Prayer in the Benedictine tradition,
and so in a Monastery of the Heart,
springs from the reflection and soul-wrestling
that brings us to the bar of our deepest selves,
seeking forgiveness, pleading for strength.

It is said in concert
with monastics of the heart everywhere,
with those for whom care for the soul
and care for the world
are always equal concerns.

Prayer is the conversion of the self-centered self
to the conscious contemplative,
to the prophetic witness
of the radical spiritual life.

In a Monastery of the Heart,
we do not pray merely to pray.

We pray to become
more a sign of the mind of God today
than we were yesterday.

The Benedictine prays
to put on the mind of God
more and more
and forever more.

The daily dinning of the Word of God
into the soul of the seeker
changes both the seeker
and the world in which the seeker
plants the Word.

There is in the Benedictine spirituality
of prayer, then,
as much a consciousness of content
as there is a choice of
prayer forms and formats.

In thirteen chapters on prayer,
the ancient Rule, in its specification
of the psalms for the day,
lays out the concepts
upon which Benedictine spirituality rests:
that good overcomes evil,
that God is our strength,
that God is present in every part of life,

that God is our refuge,
that God is merciful,
that sin is destructive of both the self
and the world,
and that praise of God is the purpose of life.

In those ideas and that consciousness
we rest,
secure in the presence of God,
certain of the love of God,
convinced that our trust in God
is never, ever in vain.

5

Silence

"Monastics should diligently cultivate silence at all times."

Silence is the mother
of the Spirit.
It births in us
the cloister of the heart.
It brings us beyond the noise
of chaos and clutter and confusion
of a spinning world
to the cool, calm center
of the spiritual self.

Silence enables us to rest in that center,
to allow God to work in us there,
to clear from our hearts
whatever thoughts or pain,
desires or demands,

clamor within us for puerile attention
and so take us away from our best selves.

In silence, we learn to listen
to others
who are also seeking God
in a Monastery of the Heart,
to hear their pain and their wisdom,
their experiences and the truths in them,
that bring our own wisdom
to light, to question, to development.

It is silence that keeps us
from giving full rein
to the empty imaginings
and cruel commentaries
always too fresh at hand
in our narcissistic selves.

"It is written," the Rule teaches,
"'In a flood of words
you will not avoid sin.'"

We are expected, invited, then,
to surrender the satisfaction
of the too sharp retort,
the too sour remark,
the too common temptation
to dishonesty

that comes with the rattle
of empty speech,
of speech that is not reflective,
of speech that wastes the depth of life
on the mundane.

In a Monastery of the Heart,
we are challenged
to exchange all those empty ideas
for the depth of reflection,
the calm of thought,
and clarity of insight
that silence brings in its wake
to the soul that longs—in silence—
for it to come.

Silence protects us from our noisy selves
and prepares us for the work of God in us.

In silence,
we come to understand ourselves.

In silence,
we become able
to hear the voice of God
calling us beyond ourselves—
always to the better,
always to the more.

———

It is of the essence, then,
that in a Monastery of the Heart
space for silence
be treasured and guarded,
sought and made sacred,
so that the spiritual life
may grow and flourish in us—
where otherwise
only the weeds of empty words
may take root.

When we make space for silence
in our lives,
we take the time
to heal what it is in us
that still simmers and burns,
hidden away—
sometimes even from ourselves—
but fierce in its perdurance
and its ability to scorch our souls
with the acids of time long past.

As the Rule reminds us, "It is written,
'The tongue holds the key
to life and death.'"

It is silence that shields us
from our first impulses
to resist changes

or reject new challenges
or rebut new ideas
or denounce the ideas
of others.

It is silence that refuses
to let us use humor to wound
or sarcasm to degrade
or criticism to demean.

"We absolutely condemn,"
the Rule teaches,
"any vulgarity and gossip
and talk leading to laughter."

Instead, silence lays us open
to possibilities,
to people,
to ideas
we would have otherwise
forever scorned.

Regular periods of solitude and silence
comfort, heal, and restore us
to ourselves—
fresh and new and quieted.
Silence prepares us for prayer.
It gives us new energy for life.
It takes us to the depth of the soul

and the mountaintop of life
to stretch our vision
and rest our souls
for the journey to God
that never ends.

The noise outside of us
is not the enemy.

It is the noise within—
our desires that plague us,
our worries that deplete us,
our thoughts that agitate us—
that we must calm.

It is the noise within
that life in a Monastery of the Heart
enables us to transcend
and to transform.

Benedictine spirituality is embedded
in both quiet and encounter,
in contemplation and community.
It is silence that is the circuit
between the two.

It is silence that prepares us
to hear God.
It is also silence

that makes fruitful the encounters
we are meant to serve
in the spirit of God.

For speech not tinged by silence,
the Rule teaches,
"we do not permit a disciple
to engage in words of that kind."

6

Prayerful Reading

"Listen readily to holy reading."

Benedictine spirituality
is not an exercise in private devotion
or personal pieties.
Benedictine prayer is not
simply ceaseless recitation
of scripture passages and psalmic verse.
It is the beginning
of a lifelong conversation with God.

To deepen that conversation,
to give it flow
and substance,
meaning and heart,
the Benedictine is to read the scriptures
and holy books,
reflect on them deeply,

and respond to them consciously
and personally
until, at long last,
we come to radiate the meaning of them
for all the world to see.

So important is this process
in Benedict's view
that he legislates the hours of the day
in which sacred, prayerful reading—
lectio—
is to take place.

"They will devote themselves
to their reading," he says,
and allows no other activity
to interfere with it.
No other activity
at all.

Most interesting, perhaps, in our day and age
when reading is a popular pastime—
and one of the most telling elements
of the Rule—
is that it is in the chapter
"The Daily Manual Labor"
where Benedict talks most directly
about the place of reading and reflection
in Benedictine life.

———

Lectio,
my own, unplumbed, personal responses
to the cycles of prayers
and readings
that make up the Liturgy of the Hours—
the daily choral prayer common
to traditional monastic life everywhere—
is to be taken seriously,
is, in fact, to be worked at.

Nothing is left to chance here.

In Benedict's time,
in a culture more illiterate than not,
in communities of peasants
and craftsmen,
shepherds and men-at-arms,
he required
the work of the mind,
the harrowing of the soul
with the ideas and sacred stories
and the words of the holy ones
who went before.

Ignorance, Benedict knows, enslaves
the soul in a regimen of substanceless devotions.
It limits our insights of a cosmic God.
It reduces the spiritual life

to a kind of pietism
that is unworthy
of the life-changing profundity
of the Gospels.

In a Monastery of the Heart,
it is lectio, prayerful reading—
my personal reflections on the words
and challenges
of scripture,
the eruptions of nature,
the vagaries of life,
the insights of poets and artists
and holy teachers—
that really stretch my soul.

It is these words
that confront my daily life
with the daily face of God.

They stir my heart
with the words of Jesus.

They bring me heart-to-heart
with the psalmist's cry
of universal pain.

Lectio demands my personal response.
It refuses to allow me

to ignore the continuing cries
of God to me,
day after day,
hour after hour,
every moment of my life.

Lectio, this careful prayerful reading,
this intense meditation and reflection
on one word, one idea at a time,
frees us from our misperceptions
about Jesus
as a figure of love without purpose,
as a doer of miracles without meaning,
as a model of personal care for others
without social concern
for society as a whole.

It is lectio that gives
the contemplative orientation
to Benedictine spirituality
in a Monastery of the Heart.

It integrates practice and meaning.

It makes the spiritual life
more than a round of exercises.
It makes it
personal and mystical,
vision-filled and prophetic.

The contemplative sees the world
as God sees the world,
because the contemplative
spends life rooted in
the kind of reading and reflection
that breaks open the heart
to the mind of God.

A spiritual life without
regular,
daily,
sacred reading and reflection
lacks the pillars
on which a lifetime
of spiritual insight
depends.

Lectio deepens the holy leisure
of silence and solitude.
It fills us with the substance we need
to be filled with the call of Jesus,
the Word of God,
and the power of the Spirit
it takes to make us
doers—and not just hearers—
of the Word.

Holy reading is the beginning

of union with God
here and now
that brings serenity,
courage,
and meaning
to everything else we do in life.

Lectio
nourishes both mind and soul
far beyond the routine
of daily prayer.
Benedictine spirituality
prods us all to grow beyond the present
to the fullness of an unknown future
that is as much mystical
as it is faithful to the daily contours of life
in a Monastery of the Heart.

7

Retreat and Reflection

"The life of a monastic ought to be a continuous Lent."

There is a time in every life
when the very act
of looking back and taking stock
becomes essential
to going forward.

Without the light
that shines out of the darkness
of the past,
we cannot chart
a new path
to the future.

Monastic spirituality
is built around
a life of retreat and reflection.

"The life of a monastic,"
Benedict writes,
"ought to be a continuous Lent"—
a life in which holy reading,
self-control,
and reflection on the great questions
of life
should be of the essence.

For those with a Benedictine heart,
a Lenten spirit
is *not* an exercise in spiritual athleticism
designed to show
that my fasting is better than
your fasting.

In a Monastery of the Heart,
the Benedictine soul
learns always to return
to the cave of the heart,
where the superfluities of life
do not distract
from the significance of life.

This requires the cultivation
of a reflective soul
and a disciplined mind
that goes regularly into "retreat"—

into that space where we look,
first of all, at what we set out to be,
and then look consciously
at what we are now doing
to get there.

Retreat time is the practice
of making personal time
for the kind of spiritual time
that is beyond the routine
of religious practices or spiritual duties.

Part of our spiritual journey,
Benedict implies,
must, if the soul is to make progress
in the spiritual life,
be spent remembering
what we say are our intentions in life,
in the light of what we can clearly see
are becoming the patterns and actions
of our lives.

In fact, what we're called to do
is to pray more thoughtfully,
to read more intensely,
to feel more keenly the distance
between what we say we are
and what we know ourselves
to be,

and to strengthen our capacity
for resolve.

Retreat times remind us
that it is easy
to become slack
in concern for the mundane,
the daily,
and the unglamourous
in the face of a world so enticingly
exciting.

Life in a Monastery of the Heart is meant
to freshen the embers
and stoke the fire
of fidelity,
to deepen our understanding
of the great treasure we seek,
to remind us of who we are
and what we are meant to be,
to bring to new life in us again
the sight of the road
on which we have put our feet.
Retreat time is the flagship piece of the year
that sets the standard
for a rhythm of life that moves seamlessly
between contemplation and action,
between work and Sabbath,
between a regular retreat

and reflection days
throughout the year.

There is a temptation in religious life
to play religious,
to dress the part of the seeker,
to look, as the Gospels warn us,
wan and worn out from fasting.

What is more growthful,
the Rule demonstrates,
is to ask ourselves regularly
about all the little ways
we are tempted to cut the corners
of the spiritual life:
by ceasing to pray,
by giving up on the study of the faith,
by failing to grapple with the scriptures,
by neglecting to go out of ourselves
to meet the needs of others,
to tell the world a Gospel truth,
to give voice to the pain of the world,
to put down the ambitions of the political,
to take up the challenges of the prophets.

Retreat times remind us
always to make the space
to begin—again—
and, in the midst of the cloying demands

of work and family,
of money-making worries
and the stressors of social systems,
to fix the eye of the heart
on the really important things
of life.

In every Monastery of the Heart,
there must be regular times
set aside
to go down
into these inner recesses of the soul
once more, alone and centered,
to take another look, a new kind of look,
at ourselves.

Retreat, reflection, Sabbath,
and soul-space
are of the essence
of the monastic spirit—
not for our sake alone
but for the sake of those
who depend on us
to make the promise of creation
new again.

First, painfully aware of our own
lack of steeled spirit,
and full of compunction—

what the ancients called
the regret of the soul—
we must forgive ourselves
for being less than
we know we can be.

Second, we must turn
the compass point of the heart
back again to where God waits for us,
arms open, full of mercy, made of love,
to be our own best selves—
not for our own sake alone
but for the sake of the rest of the world.

Benedictine spirituality, after all,
is life lived to the hilt.
It is a life of concentration
on life's ordinary dimensions.
It is an attempt to do
the ordinary things of life
extraordinarily well.

OUR COMMUNITY

8

Mutuality

"We intend to establish a school for God's service. We hope to set down nothing harsh, nothing burdensome."

Community is a matter
of the heart
and the mind.
It cannot be created
by place alone,
and it cannot be destroyed
by distance alone.

It is of the essence
of the soul.

What we identify with,
what gives us a sense of purpose,
of belonging,
of support
is our community.

In the Rule of Benedict,
community is made up of
common worship,
common ownership,
and common life.

It is about drinking from
the same well of belief
and giving myself
to the same life goals,
and aims,
and objectives
as those with whom I have promised
to make this journey.

It is about having little or nothing
of my own, on the one hand,
and having a right
to everything the community owns,
on the other.

It cannot be accomplished
without making some kind
of connections—
but connections alone
are no guarantee
that a real community
will really form.

On the other hand,
to become community
in a Monastery of the Heart
requires regular
and meaningful interaction
among the members.
It is more than calendrical
or routine celebrations,
as important as these are,
for the building
of a common spirit.

It is the process of creating
and sharing common bonds:
the faith life that underpins a group,
the personal life and affections
of each member,
the emotional life that forms
and fluctuates and drives each of us
at different levels
at different times,
and the undercurrents and ideas and concepts
that stir our attitudes and hopes
for the human enterprise.

Community always means
that we're in this together.
And, if we're lucky, it means

that the group knows us well enough
to be happy that we're there.

Community is the backdrop against which
we do what we do.
It gives us the underpinning
that enables us to go on
when we're tired,
to go forward
when we're afraid,
to go more deeply into the unmasking
of the self
when everything inside of us
seems to have gone to stone,
goes dry and dull
and lethargic.

Community building does not just happen.
It cannot be taken for granted.
It requires both great faith
and great trust
that is generated by a continuing display
of great human care
that begins with me,
and then comes back to me.

It takes a great deal of energy
to create community.
And in today's world,

community takes many shapes.

The kind of community for which
the ancient Rule of Benedict is written,
is based on a great deal
of common physical presence.

But as the world enlarges,
so does the concept of community.
The physical is still important—
but differently.
Now community is often virtual,
but just as real in many dimensions
as sitting next to the same person
in chapel our entire lives.

In a Monastery of the Heart,
what is important is
that we each be an extension
of the Gospel,
and an extension of each other,
and an extension of Benedictine spirituality
at the same time.

What is imperative is that the sharing
of the common mind
be just as important
as once was the sharing
of a common schedule,

or a common dormitory,
or a common work.

What is central is that together
we use our goods
for something greater than ourselves,
that we "do not store up grain in barns,"
as the scriptures say,
for our own security alone,
but use the profits of our labor
for the good of others, as well.

It is a process of making
all of human community real,
and of doing it
out of a common vision
and one heart,
in whatever form is available—
so that the spirit of community
that is Benedictine to its core
may spread like a holy plague
throughout the world.

9

Equality

"Monastics keep their rank in the monastery according to the date of their entry and the virtue of their lives."

We like to think that equality
is the basic characteristic
of this—our—period of history.

Ironically, inequality is the great sign
of our time.

Today, everyone is supposed to be able
to get ahead, to have the same rights,
to be equally protected under the law,
to have the same opportunities
as everyone else.

But it is also our world
that enslaves the poor to the drudgery

of survival,
that ranks women as lower human beings
than men,
that distributes the goods
we produce
according to race,
that worships at the feet
of the gods of money,
and lives in gated communities
in order to keep
the rest of the world out.

To this world,
Benedictine spirituality says clearly,
"No."

Not race, not age, not money,
not class, not gender
determine the nature
of a Benedictine community.
There is no status here.

We keep our rank
in the monastery,
the Rule says,
based on the date of our entry
and the virtue of our lives.

Those who are older in life,

those who have borne the heat of the day
longer, more intensely, more consistently,
are the community's elders,
its wisdom figures,
its spiritual icons,
its signs that life grows sweeter with time,
that life grows holier with experience,
that life grows richer of heart
as the heart grows deeper into God.

But age and seniority
are also not its gods.
The Rule writes,
according to scripture,
"Absolutely nowhere
shall age automatically determine rank.
Remember that Samuel and Daniel
were still boys
when they judged their elders."

In a Benedictine community,
there is no ranking of people
by any social criteria,
regardless of the norms
of any other organization
around it.

In a Benedictine community,
we are all equal at the table—

even when the direction of the community itself
is at stake.

"As often as anything important
is to be done in the monastery,"
the Rule reads,
"the prioress or abbot
shall call the whole community together . . .
the Spirit often reveals what is better
to the younger."

The principle is a clear one:
"The Spirit blows where it will."
We cannot damp down
the fire of the Spirit
on the basis of anything
but the greater movement
of the Spirit itself.

It is from this perspective
that a Benedictine
looks at the world
and lives in it,
and works in it,
and plans for it.

In the Benedictine heart
no door is closed,

no lines are drawn.

In a Monastery of the Heart, as well,
whoever else makes enemies
of differences,
the seeker listens ever harder
to learn what differences
have to teach,
what otherness has to say.

Benedictine spirituality takes in difference
and makes it its own.

Equality is the very ground
of mutual obedience.
Neither age, nor race, nor sex
is a valid measure of wisdom.
Benedictine communities,
based on equality,
deliver us from social bias
and groundless prejudices.

As a result,
a Monastery of the Heart
must be based
on mutual respect
and grounded
in mutual affection.

———

It is this that makes "community"—
however it is formed,
and meets,
and prays together,
and seeks the good as one.

It is "community"
that makes the monastery
as human as it is holy—
and as holy as it is human.

Equality does not interrupt
the presentation of ideas
that others offer the group.
It does not demean them
or disparage them
or mock them or deride them.
It does not dismiss easily or idly
the insights, the concerns,
the questions or the answers of the other.

It does not build walls around the heart.

Equality, the offshoot of humility,
sees in the face of the other—
all others—
the face of God.

Without it, no group,

and no Monastery of the Heart,
can ever be really sure
that whatever it thinks it knows
about the spiritual life
it really knows fully.

10

Direction and Counsel

*"Do everything with counsel and you will not
be sorry afterward."*

Benedictine spirituality sets out
to build communities
that, together, seek the universal God,
that hold the wounded of the world
in one heart,
and that serve the world
by being for it
oases of peace and prayer,
beacons of truth and justice.

To do this in a Monastery of the Heart,
where coming to know one another intimately
requires more than the routine
of a daily schedule,
takes distinct and regular effort.

It requires that we explore
and support
the gifts of each
in conscious
and committed ways.

It demands that we work together
to release one another's gifts
to strengthen the communal voice.

It insists that the ideas of each
must be both solicited and respected,
that the needs of each must be met,
and that the energies of all
must be put in the service
of the whole community.

None of that can be done totally alone.
All of that requires mutual support.

Clearly, then, Monasteries of the Heart,
like all Benedictine communities
of whatever structure and shape,
are not loose confederations
of independent individuals.

Neither are they
monarchies in which individuals,

in the name of holiness,
are expected to give up
both their right
to have their voices heard
and their responsibility
to speak their truths.

But it does mean that the community
binds itself together
for the sake of learning from
the wisdom of all.

Leaders exist to facilitate
the community's efforts to do
all these things
wisely, warmly, and well.

Where and when leadership emerges,
as leadership always does—
officially or unofficially—
it must be exercised for and with
the direction of the group.

It is in choosing our counselors
and identifying our leaders
that we each take our own soul
in our hands.

It is easy to choose as leaders
those who claim to have answers

we do not want to trouble ourselves
with discovering.
Better to simply follow orders,
we are tempted to believe,
than to make the effort
to participate in the hard, slow process
of determining for ourselves,
alone or together,
what is the holiest of holy possibilities
in the sight of God.

What is dishonest
is to choose for leaders those
who allow the community
to drift into nice, comfortable, secure routines
that pass for holiness
but, if truth were known,
secretly mask a community's resistance
to spiritual growth.

The complacent community
asks itself no difficult questions
that might require new efforts to answer.

The comfortable community
opens no new or challenging paths
that might bring down
criticism on the system
in which they exist.

The self-satisfied community
carves out no new directions,
risks no new questions,
that might disturb the sleepy apathy
that comes to anyone over time.

The placid community
foregoes its prophetic role
to live the God-life in the midst
of the profane
and chooses instead leaders
who maintain the system
in the spirit of the past,
but do little or nothing
to stretch it to the full height
and breadth and depth of itself.

The Rule of Benedict
is clear about the nature
of the leaders for which we must look:

Leaders must be an example
to the community of its best self:
open, loving, hospitable;
committed to the study of the Word;
kind and understanding of the struggles we all face
on the way to the holy emptiness of self
that is full only of God.

The leader "must point out . . .
all that is good and holy
more by example than by words,"
the Rule teaches.

The leader must value the Gospel
beyond public approval.

The leader must be committed
to the needs and growth of community,
and even-handed in their love
for the members.
Let the leader, the Rule says,
"avoid all favoritism in the monastery."

The leader must maintain the integrity
of the community
and encourage it to be what it is meant to be:
a sign of the world to come,
a bringer of peace,
a haven for the homeless,
the heart of the temple
on the streets of the city,
a light in the dark to those
who seek peace and justice
and human community.

Identifying and choosing good leaders

is of the essence of
community building.
We will become what
we choose.

If we choose to be a Monastery of the Heart
where love casts out fear,
we must choose those as leaders
who know how to embrace
with wisdom and truth
friend and stranger alike.

If we choose to be a justice-seeking
Monastery of the Heart,
we must choose those
who are willing to risk themselves publicly
for the sake of the Gospel.

If we choose to be a peace-making
Monastery of the Heart,
we must choose those
who can find in differences
the very breadth of God.

More, whatever the choices
made around us,
in a world of competing interests,
we must always,
as individuals,

choose those to follow
whose lives have been lived
with love and justice,
with open arms,
and with hearts that beat for the poor.

All Monasteries of the Heart must bring
their personal influence wherever they are—
in the community itself
and through their presence
in the world at large—
to lead the way toward justice
for the sake of the world.

We must seek our counsel
and direction
from those who forever
put the God-life
above everything else,
including the systems
in which they live.
And, most of all,
we must be faithful
to immersion in the Spirit
and open to the presence of God
in the mind and soul
of the community.

11

Sufficiency and Sharing

"Do everything with moderation."

The purpose of the monastic life is never
to amass wealth
for the sake of the self.

Instead, Benedict's definition
of the relationship between persons
and things
is sufficiency, not frugality.

Benedictine spirituality does not see indigence,
abject poverty, stringency,
and parsimoniousness
as a lifestyle to be desired,
let alone a high-level signal of holiness.

The monastic ideal is about the ability
to understand the difference

between need and want,
between having what is necessary
rather than doing without what is necessary—
simply for the sake of doing without.

Those who follow
the Benedictine way
understand
the personal impact
and social import
of what it means, in a starving world,
to "hold all things in common."

In a world where the accumulation
of goods, money, power, and property
denies millions the basics of life—
their wages, their resources, their education,
their health, their future—
Benedictine spirituality
confronts that kind of engorgement
with the principle
of sufficiency.

"It is written," the Rule says,
"Distribution was made as
each had need."
And, "Whoever needs less
should thank God
and not be distressed,

but whoever needs more
should feel humble
because of their weakness . . ."

It is not the *use* of the goods
required to make contemporary life possible—
cars, computers, electronics, telephones—
that is the measure
of poverty for the Benedictine heart.
It is the over-consumption—
the unmitigated greed
that drives a person
to have in undue measure
what others have little or nothing of,
to want for the self rather than for humanity—
that is the distinction between
Benedictine poverty
and being poor.

Benedictine poverty does not require us
to refuse to have money,
or earn a salary,
or support ourselves
"as our ancestors did."

On the contrary,
it simply confines us
to what is necessary—
so that we can help to sustain

those who cannot earn
the money they need
to take care
of themselves.

In a world where the scales of wealth
tip precipitously toward
the West, the white, the male,
and the few at the top everywhere,
it is Benedictine spirituality that
refuses to give in
to the acquisitiveness and amassing of goods.

It's the delusion of having to have at our disposal
ten kinds of potato chips,
thirty pair of shoes,
the biggest and best of everything,
that, in the end, wars against the desire
of the heart
to live a simple life.

In a Monastery of the Heart,
seekers live
with one eye on the needs
of everyone else
as well as their own.

When we find that we have
accumulated good things

in multiples
and use few of them ever,
it is time to give some of them away
to those who have none.

It is not necessary to look poor
to live a simple life.
But it is necessary to love simplicity,
to gather only what is necessary for ourselves,
not necessarily to have the best,
the most, the latest, or the most expensive,
let alone to have all there is
of anything.

In a Monastery of the Heart,
the commitment to the development
of Benedict's concept of community
must be far wider
in this century than it was in the sixth.
It must burst through
the monastery gates into a world
where national laws
and local prejudices
fail to take into account
the effects of our over-consumption
of food, energy, resources, and weaponry
on those who find themselves hungry,
empty-handed, and sick.

———

In a Monastery of the Heart,
we must begin to define community globally
rather than simply locally,
and work at every level to make it so.
We must see the moderation of consumption
as our way to reach beyond the boundaries
of our own lives
to the obscenely poor—
who stand outside looking in
at our three-car garages
and second homes
and wish for simply enough
of what we have
to live a humanely human life themselves.

12

Nourishment

"Nothing is so inconsistent with the life of the
monastic as overindulgence."

The seeker's ideal
is to be "in the world
but not of it"—
to be like everyone else
but different where it counts.

For those who seek to define
this *other* quality of life
by membership
in a Monastery of the Heart,
the relationship between
what it means to belong to both
the world around us
and the monastery
is an especially important one.

How, for instance, shall we
eat and drink as monastics of the heart
in a world half-starving on one hand,
and meant to be enjoyed
on the other?

How does Benedictine spirituality
define our attitude
toward matters of the body?

Whatever its stress on communal welfare,
the Rule of Benedict
is very much attuned
to individual differences.
Nowhere is it clearer on that point
than in the chapters on
the proper amount of food and drink.

In an era still attuned to desert monks,
with all their asceticisms
and strict dietary rules,
the community lifestyle
of Benedict of Nursia
never foregoes its rejection
of extreme asceticisms,
practices which are often
a source of spiritual pride,
and always a source of spiritual distraction.

Benedictinism understands
that differences are the strength
of every community—
and the challenge.

"It is, therefore, with some uneasiness,"
Benedict says in the Rule,
"that we specify
the amount of food and drink
for others."

And he doesn't.
Instead he legislates for choice
and for personal comfort.

He warns against gluttony
and drunkenness
but he allows wine, for instance,
"with due regard for the infirmities of the sick,"
and requires that at least
"two kinds of cooked food"
be served at every meal,
so that no one went hungry
in a culture where monastics
were expected to be abstemious.

"If fruit or fresh vegetables are available,"
the Rule continues,

"a third dish may also be added."
And except for the very sick,
Benedict wants all to
"abstain entirely from eating
the meat
of four-footed animals."

What are we to think of these guidelines
in a culture of excess
here and now?

Is it "religious," "holy," "spiritual"
to be fed with care
and trusted to know when enough
is enough?
Is it monastic to live on anything
but bread and water?

The answer is a plain one
in the context of the Rule:
sanctity is not about excess
of *any* kind,
not the physical,
not even the spiritual.

It is about dealing with
all the good things of life
in moderation,

properly,
appropriately.

A study of human nature,
and an awareness of the gift of the senses,
makes the conclusion clear:
restraint
is just as holy
as self-abnegation—
maybe, in some instances,
more so.

We do not become holy
on food and drink—
either the kind we eat and drink,
or the kind we do not.

Holiness is made of sterner stuff
than that—
however much great fasting
may impress the world
with our purported sanctity.

Benedict says,
"We read that monastics
should not drink wine at all,
but since the monastics of our day
cannot be convinced of this,
let us at least agree to drink moderately,

and not to the point of excess,
for 'wine makes even the wise go astray.'"

It is not the wine,
it is the "falling off"
that is the problem.
It is the ability
to set limits for ourselves—
and keep them.
It is the ability
to meet the standards
of the highest level
of human development
that is the mark of the truly monastic soul.

Benedictine spirituality
is a spirituality based on the awareness
that everyone—
to work, to enjoy life,
to concentrate on more than
their appetites—
needs the staples of life.

Benedictine communities in the Middle Ages
made the fields flush with crops
and taught peasants to farm
so that everyone in the area—
nobility, merchants, and peasants—
could all live without fear of starvation,

could feed their children
and sustain their families.

In our day and age, then,
when joblessness and low wages,
high costs and limited opportunities,
plague families everywhere
and on all levels,
to be spiritual, the Rule warns us,
we, too, must be most concerned
with those who do not have food and staples,
and be just as committed
as our ancestors in the faith
to seeing that the hungry around us, too,
are also full.

In a Monastery of the Heart,
we learn from the Rule and the tradition
that what we enjoy for ourselves,
we must supply for others, as well.

Benedictine spirituality
does not depend on symbolic actions
as the hallmark of its quality.
It requires us to do
every tangible thing we can
to create a human community—
as decent and as humanly dignified
as our own.

OUR SERVICE

13

Good Work

*"When they live by the labor of their hands, then
they are really monastics."*

Prayer and contemplation,
Benedict is clear,
are no substitute for work.
Nor are they an excuse
to detach ourselves
from the holy act of human responsibility
for making the world go round.

The simple truth is
that sloth is not a Benedictine virtue.
Work for the sake
of hastening the coming of the Reign of God
is every bit as much a part
of Benedictine life
as prayer times and holy reading.

In fact, it is not just any work—
employment, engagement,
usefulness—
with which the Rule
is concerned.
It is "the daily manual labor,"
the work of the hands,
the kind of work that makes things happen.

To avoid manual labor
entirely
is to participate in the cultivation
of a classist or racist or sexist society—
in which some of us
do the *really* significant things of life,
and others of us
do the physical work the rest of us think
we are too important
to do.

Whatever our motives might be,
to absent ourselves from manual labor
is to participate in the creation
of a servant society
in which we give ourselves
the right not to serve.

But Benedictine spirituality is about

equality and community,
about service and mutual support.
And that takes many forms,
not simply one.
The Benedictine heart knows that
simply staying close
to the mechanical functions
of what it means to get through a day—
running the vacuum,
washing the dishes,
shoveling the snow,
doing the laundry,
peeling the vegetables,
cleaning out the car,
making the bed,
bathing the children—
keeps us all, men and women,
aware of the struggles
embedded in every dimension of life.

It also keeps us in touch with one another,
with those we love
and whose love carries us
in all the small, hidden little ways
we barely notice—
but cannot do without.

It makes us aware of the burdens
carried by those around us,

in the family and the neighborhood,
whose full lives
we would otherwise never know.

It gives us a sense of what it means
to be a fully human human being,
rather than a foreigner
in our own homes,
an outlander in our own society.

That kind of shared work
makes a family a family
and a community a community,
rather than a mere way station or rest home
for some of us—
thanks to the full-time obligations
of others of us
to service the physical world that enables us
to go on functioning.

But manual labor in today's society
is no longer—
in much of the West, at least—
a full-time occupation.
Meals come packaged now.
Housecleaning is
either mechanized or simplified.
Industry has, in large part,
given way to services,

and physical labor to technology.

We live in a time, then,
when the work we do is not nearly
as important as knowing *why* we do it.

For the Benedictine spirit,
work is not simply work.
Whatever kind of work it is—
professional or technical,
physical or intellectual,
financial or social—
it is to be *good* work,
work that makes the world
a better, more just, more fair,
and more humane place
for everyone.

"Idleness is the enemy of the soul,"
the Rule reminds us.

That insight bears pondering.

The truth is that work has
a spiritual function.
It is done for the sake of the soul,
not for the punishment of the body
or for the gratification of the ego.
Good work is meant to build into us

a respect for the order and beauty
that the cultivation of the spiritual life
demands.

Good work is a human being's
contribution to the development
of humankind
and the fulfillment of the universe.

In fact, why we work
is the very bedrock of Benedictine spirituality.
It is about the bringing
of the Reign of God on earth.

It is about
completing the work of God
in the upbuilding of the world.

Whatever the Benedictine does—
mop the floor, weed the garden, fold the clothes,
write the reports, plan the programs, produce the goods—
becomes an act of human liturgy
in praise of
what it is to be alive,
to redeem creation from chaos
and our souls from apathy.

Work that participates in a common project of humanity
frees us from total self-centeredness

and makes us a prouder, more fulfilled part
of the human race.

Whatever work we do—
even if it does not pertain directly to the poor or the needy,
the traumatized and dispossessed—
it is work that gives us the means of reaching with alms
the hurting places of humanity,
to which our lives are grafted
simply by our being alive.

Work, in Benedictine spirituality,
calls for labor—
manual labor,
spiritual labor,
and intellectual labor—
that continues the co-creation
of the world.

In the end, they are all part
of the same condition,
the same scriptural mandate
"to till the garden and keep it"
that is at the heart of Benedictine life.

It is all to be good work,
in the tradition
of the great Benedictine monasteries
before us

that rebuilt Europe
after the fall of the Roman Empire,
that saved culture
and preserved learning in the Middle Ages.

Monasteries of the Heart in our own time
must, as virtual communities,
as committed individuals,
define the social labor—
the peacemaking, the culture creating,
the justice making, the community building—
by which they shall personally or corporately be known.

Work is a path toward self-fulfillment, as well.
We become better at something in ourselves—
more skilled, more creative, more effective—
when we work.
We discover that, indeed, we are
good for something.

Good work is, at the same time,
its own kind of asceticism.
It needs no symbolic rituals or contrived penances.
The very act of continuing something
until we succeed at it
is soul-searing, life-changing enough.

Work also puts us in solidarity with those
for whom the rewards of labor

are few and far between.
It keeps us conscious
of the burdens of the poor,
of injustice to workers,
of the dignity of human labor,
of the glory of ongoing creation.

It makes us equal partners
with the rest of the human race
in this one common human endeavor
to grow the globe to wholeness.

Good work is our gift to the future.
It is what we leave behind—
our persistence, our precision,
our commitment,
our fidelity to the smallest and meanest of tasks—
that will change the mind
of generations to come
about our sacred obligation
to bear our share of
the holy-making enterprise that is work.

Then we shall truly be
authentic witnesses to the fact
that a life lived in the scriptures
shapes a universal heart
and rallies the global soul.

———

Then it will be clear that the spiritual life
is not an escape from the world,
it is a commitment to share with the world
the creative potential
of the monastic vision
of life.

A Monastery of the Heart
stands as sign to the world
that whatever work we do
will be done with full heart
and extra effort,
not for our own sake alone
but for the sake
of the development of the entire world.

14

Co-Creation

*"Regard all utensils and goods of the monastery as
sacred vessels of the altar."*

Benedictine spirituality
is a sacramental spirituality.
It holds all things—
the earth and all its goods—
as sacred.

In our twenty-first-century view of life—
through the lens of the Rule of Benedict—
we know now in new ways
that the earth and all its fruits
are not for our exploitation,
they are for our care.
We are co-creators with God
of what creation has left unfinished.
What has been left in embryo

is left for us to develop.
What can be developed
God trusts us to bring to full potential.

But not for ourselves alone.

Co-creation,
the human commitment
to continue the work of God
on earth,
requires us to tend the land
and conserve the waters,
to till the garden
and protect the animals,
to use the things of the earth
in ways that enhance all life now—
and preserve them
for later generations, as well.

The human-centered view of creation
is a stunted one.
It fails to recognize the *oneness* of creation,
the symphony of life forms
that depend on one another
to bring the universe,
pulsing and throbbing with life,
to a wholeness that is mutual,
that reflects the full face of God
rather than simply our own.

The male-centered view of creation
is an incomplete, an inadequate one.
It fails to recognize women
as equal agents
in the development of creation
and so ignores half the resources of creation
in the decision-making process
of life.

Benedictine spirituality seeks a balanced life,
one in harmony with all its parts—
earth, fire, air, and water,
animals, plants, females, and males—
all alive in the heart of God.

To allow ourselves to become
digital chips in an electronic world,
isolates in an interdependent universe,
women and men out of touch
with the life pulse of a living God,
indifferent to creation,
concerned only with ourselves,
and still call ourselves good—
is to mistake the rituals of religion
for the sanctifying dimensions of spirituality.

In a Monastery of the Heart
we are called to listen to nature

as well as to one another,
to hear its groans
and till its gardens,
to nurture its young
and maintain the purity of its air,
until we ourselves become
the voices for life in everything
everywhere.

To do that we must become part
of the liturgy of life,
treating as holy everything we touch,
regarding as sacred every being alive,
intent on preserving
the best of what is—
while we use our science and technology
to protect, defend, and enhance them all.

To pursue the path
of Benedictine spirituality means
that we will leave
whatever part of the world we inhabit—
its neighborhoods and nations,
its oceans and preserves,
its forests and its soil—
in better condition than they were
before we came.

Benedictines over the centuries,

following the life the Rule prescribes,
laid the foundation of the towns
to which they brought order and organization,
hospices, learning, scripture, and art,
the tools of civilization,
and the sustenance of the soul.

They used every human form
of education and skill
to bring order out of chaos,
equality to the masses,
and healing to the globe.

They tilled arid land and made it green.
They dried the swamps and made them flower.

They hired the peasants
and taught them new skills.

They seeded Europe with crops
that sustained entire populations,
they raised the cattle that fed and clothed,
they plowed the land,
they distilled liquors and brewed beer
that brought joy to the heart
and health to the body,
and they did all of that
despite the plundering and pillaging
that went on around them

as the forces of war and domination
overran and burned down
one defenseless region
after another.

It is not possible to live life
in a Monastery of the Heart
and fail to nurture the seeds of life
for every living creature,
every way, everywhere.

It is on the altar of creation
that we celebrate our Benedictine spirituality,
as our ancestors have done before us
for over 1,500 years.

15

Loving Care

"Let those who are not strong have help . . ."

Patience and care
are two pillars
of Benedictine community.

They hold up before our eyes,
in blinding light,
in immovable form,
what is to be
the nature of our presence
in the world.

There is in Benedictine spirituality
a deeply compassionate heart
that neither glorifies the suppression
of human feelings
nor denies the reality of human needs.

Nowhere is that clearer than in
the attention the Rule gives
to the needs of the elderly, the sick,
and the children of the monastery.

Nowhere is it more important
than in a Monastery of the Heart,
which is not designed to take people
out of the arena of normal human relationships
as much as it is intended
to leaven them with a Benedictine view
of life.

Benedictine spirituality is not the kind
of religious rigor
that strips the human experience
of its humanity
in the name of the spiritual life.

With all its regulations and recommendations,
the Rule's most basic themes
are the understanding of limits,
the acceptance of our differences,
and the expectation of mutual support.

Benedictine spirituality
is not a race to win the most "spiritual points"
for strict silence,
or the spiritual athleticism of lengthy fasts,

or even perfect attendance at prayer.

Benedictine spirituality
is a community-minded game
of no-one-loses.

Whatever our boundaries or barriers,
we will help one another
over the finishing lines of life together.

We are here to enable one another
to go further.
We are here to learn from the insights
of the other.
We are here to bring all of humanity
to fullness of life.

The Rule is clear about the lengths
to which a Benedictine goes
to sustain the elderly,
to heal the sick,
to support the young in the community.

"The prioress or abbot should be extremely careful,"
the Rule teaches,
"that they suffer no neglect."

Caretakers are named,
special accommodations are provided,

diets beyond the common fare of the monastery
are given,
and "the sick may take baths
whenever it is advisable,"
Benedict says—in a time
when bathing was a luxury,
not a social necessity.

Suffering is not glorified in this Rule.
Loving care is its norm.

Children and the elderly, it declares,
"should be treated
with kindly consideration."

The very humanity of a Rule
designed
to shape a spiritual life
is a fundamental spiritual message of its own.

Life is not a regimen to be endured.
It is an enterprise
meant to be made possible,
made beautiful,
at every stage.

The message to the sick,
on the other hand,

is a spiritual discipline for us all.
"Let them not by their excessive demands
distress anyone who serves them.
Still, the sick must be patiently borne with,
because serving them
leads to a greater reward."

We are, in all instances,
to be patient in our requests,
and caring—gentle—in our concern
for others.

No amount of special asceticism
can equal the amount
of spiritual growth
and human maturity
that comes with care for others.
At the same time,
healthy disregard for the unceasing
demands of the self
is itself a sign of good mental health.

For the monastic of the heart who lives alone,
Benedictine spirituality requires
an outreach to those
in the family, the neighborhood,
the community
whose needs are being neglected.

———

For the seeker who belongs to
a Monastery of the Heart,
it calls for attention to children,
regular interaction with the elderly,
and care for those whose conditions
limit their own participation
in the community.

Whatever the situation,
whatever the group,
the seeker
in a Monastery of the Heart
is called
to build community
with the entire community.

"Whose feet will the hermit wash?"
St. Basil asks,
and the Benedictine answers,
"Everyone's."

16

Responsibility

*"Let everyone receive help as the size of the community
or local conditions warrant."*

Benedictine spirituality is communal.
It never intends
to create a world of isolates,
even for the isolated.
It sets out to gather the world
into one great common cause of two dimensions—
union with God,
and global identification
with all the human community.

A Monastery of the Heart, then,
must be a vision of life
with God at the center
and people in its heart.
To ignore one or the other,

however good
each separate one might be,
is to ignore
the very diastolic-systolic rhythm of the life.
Neither without the other is whole.

Nowhere is that clearer
than in the Rule's continual concern
for the effects of structures
on the people who must maintain them.

Seekers who live in the midst
of the world community,
obliged to its institutions,
in the service of its goals,
immersed in its systems and values,
must take to it
a different way of being in the world.

Over and over again,
in great ways and small,
Benedict calls us
to treat the rest
of the world
with respect,
with tenderness,
with understanding.

"Necessary items are to be requested

and given at the proper times,
so that no one may be disquieted or distressed,"
the Rule says.

Do not burden the infirmary staff
with unnecessary demands,
the Rule advises.

"Do not crush the bruised reed,"
the Rule says to the abbot and prioress.

"Let everyone receive help
as the size of the community
or local conditions warrant,"
the Rule recommends.

Without doubt, a Benedictine community,
a Monastery of the Heart,
does not take as its standards
the ways of corporate authority
or the norms of institutional expectations.

Here we are required always
to put the person first.

Where we are needed
at any given moment
is where we are meant to be.
The responsibility to carry

the human community
does not depend on any single person
at any single time.
It depends every bit as much
on the attitudes and support and help
of those who are being carried,
those for whose benefit the work
is being done.

Hours do not count.
I am not off duty ever
from the needs of others.

I am not allowed to ignore
the stress and burdens of others,
just because what they are doing
is not my responsibility.

This is not a 40-hour-a-week life.
My work exists wherever I see others
who are overburdened
or forever overworked.

Not everyone must do everything,
but everyone must do
something
that benefits the group
as a whole.

———

And we must do whatever we do
with total commitment
and a complete sense of responsibility.

We do not play at
being monastics of the heart.

We do not posture at
believing that every work is holy.

We do not pretend to
see God in everything
and everyone.

We are at the disposal
of the human race,
in whatever form or function
it presents itself to us:
as neighbor,
as family,
as citizen,
as stranger,
as artist,
as disciples together
on the way to God.

We are each a part of the soul
of the group,
knowing that what we do or do not do

may not hurt us personally
but will surely affect
the very future of the community.

And then each of us,
we know,
will also receive from the others
everything we, too, need
to be our best selves.

Benedictine service is not slave labor.
It is the open-handed gift
of those around us,
who know our limits
as well as their own,
and put their shoulders next to ours
to make life good
and happy,
holy and heartfelt
for everyone.

Benedictine spirituality
is not built on a mentality
of paid service for
contracted hours.

Nor is it built by placing
unending expectations
on the willing.

It is built on the trust
that each of us
will lay our lives down for the other,
as Jesus did,
and count everything we do
as the privilege of participating
in the co-creation
of the world.

For that we pray daily,
"O God, come to my assistance,
O God, make haste to help me."

Knowing that we, too,
are at least part
of everyone else's answer
to that prayer.

17

Hospitality

"Once guests have been announced, meet them with
all the courtesy of love."

It is possible, of course,
to make community
out of "our kind of people,"
out of people who look like us
and think like us
and have the same backgrounds we do.

But that is not
the kind of community
the ancient Rule
has in mind
or a Monastery of the Heart
sets out to be.

And with good cause.

When Benedict of Nursia began
his new way of living
in wild, licentious, sixth-century Rome,
he turned that world upside down.

He took into his monastic community
the rich and the poor,
the slave and the free,
the young and the old,
artists and craftsmen,
peasants and noblemen.
It was a motley crew.

And then, as if that weren't enough,
he opened the doors
of the monastery
to anyone who came,
at any time,
to anyone who knocked,
no matter who they were
or where they had been in life
along the way.

Most of all, he made of their coming
a royal affair.

Guests were to be met by
the entire community

"united in peace,"
with prayer and always
with the kiss of peace.

Benedict's community met everyone,
whoever they were,
with friendship and trust and honor.
The pilgrim,
the poor,
and the stranger
all became new royalty
at the monastery door.

"Jesus,"
the Rule teaches,
"is to be welcomed in them."

For the sake of welcome,
community silence
was broken,
the table was set,
and the abbot
ate with the guest.

"Great care and concern
are to be shown,"
the Rule goes on,
"in receiving poor people

and pilgrims because in them
more particularly
Jesus is received."

The point is clear:
the guest, to the Benedictine, is much more
than simply another social contact.

Guests, the unknown and the wandering other,
are the final
and authentic addition
to any Benedictine community.

Without them,
the very notion of Benedictine community
is suspect,
is nothing but more of the same.
Without the guest
we make the community life
all about us alone.

Families that concentrate
only on themselves
do not build up
the entire human family.

The Benedictine,
on the other hand,
is actually on the lookout for guests—

for their needs,
for their wisdom.

Like Abraham, whose desert tent was open
on all four sides
for fear a traveler might be missed,
the Benedictine community
takes special care
to make itself available
to the needs of the world.

"At the door of the monastery,"
the Rule reads,
"place a sensible person."

"This porter will need a room
near the entrance
so that visitors will always
find someone there to answer them,"
the Rule reads.
"As soon as anyone knocks
or a poor person calls out,
the porter will reply,
'Thanks be to God.'"

Thank God, you've come,
Benedictine spirituality says
to the stranger—
disturb our perfect lives.

Without guests, life here
is just one more instance
of securing ourselves in the midst of
our people, our kind, our type.

But the guest refuses to allow us
to become snug and secure
in our little monastic cells.

The guest intrudes on our schedules
and makes demands on our energy
and pries open our closed minds
and stretches our hearts
to the breaking point.

The guest refuses to allow us to see
the spiritual life as an exercise
in making neat and tidy schedules
for ourselves.

Guests save us from counting
as holiness
the ironclad world of the self
we have managed to construct and structure
so well.

Guests bring us God
in the guise of the immediate

and the urgent,
the uncomfortable
and the unknown.

They expose our emptiness of heart
and total self-centeredness,
when we may not even know ourselves
that it exists.

The guest in Benedictine spirituality
is a visit from the God of Surprises
who comes upon us
at our most vulnerable
and breaks us open
to a new part of ourselves
as well as to the needs of the other.

Guests bring the world in,
place it at our feet,
and dare us to be
who and what we say we are.
They are a blatant sign
for all to see
that any group that calls itself
a Monastery of the Heart—
but exists
only for itself and its own kind—
is really not a real community
at all.

—

A Monastery of the Heart
is a community with stretchable,
permeable,
illimitable boundaries
made up of anyone who happens
to come into it
at any time,
and always saying,
"We are here for you."

OUR PROMISE

18

A Listening Heart

*"Listen carefully to my instructions . . . and attend to
them with the ear of your heart."*

There is a magnet in a seeker's heart
whose true north is God.
It bends toward the Voice of God
with the ear of the heart
and, like sunflowers in the sun,
turns all of life toward
the living of the Word.

This listening heart is pure of pride
and free of arrogance.
It seeks wisdom—
everywhere, at all times—
and knows wisdom by the way
it echoes
the call of the scriptures.

The compass for God implanted
in the seeker's heart
stretches toward truth
and signals the way to justice.

It is attuned to the cries
of the poor and oppressed
with a timbre that allows
no interruption,
no smothering
of the Voice of God
on their behalf.

These seekers hear the voice of God
in the cry of the poor and oppressed,
and they "immediately put aside
their own concerns"
and follow God's call
in their actions.

Monastics cling to the community
in order to know a wisdom not their own,
to discover the tradition
on which they stand,
to heed the Word of God together
with one heart and one mind—
embedded in many shapes and forms,
and brought to the fullness

of God's will for them
in mind, heart, and soul.

They give themselves
to mutual obedience
in order to create a common voice—
a communal voice—
that can be heard above
the clamors of self-centeredness.
And they do the hard work
of community-living and decision-making together,
"not cringing or sluggish or half-hearted,
but free from any grumbling
or any reaction of unwillingness"—
so that none of the actions
taken together
are done in vain,
so that the Reign of God can come sooner
because we have been here.

In a Monastery of the Heart,
Benedictine listening
honors the function of leadership
to point us in the direction of truth,
but knows that neither dependence
nor license
nor authoritarianism
are a valid substitute
for communal discernment,

for seeking truth
in the light of one another's wisdom.

Communal discernment is a holy hearing
of prophetic voices among us.
It comes out of listening
to others
and responding to them
in the name of God,
so that as a community
we can move forward together,
one heart at a time.

Benedictine spirituality requires careful listening
and responding
to the Word of God,
to the call of the Jesus who leads us,
and to the call of the community
that is the foundation of our spiritual life.

It is not an obedience that rests
on blessed ignorance,
or infantile dependence,
or reckless irresponsibility,
or military authoritarianism,
or blind submission
in the name of holiness.

A truly listening heart knows

that we lose the chance for truth
if we give another—any other—
either too much, or too little,
control over the conscience
that is meant to be ours alone.

And yet, at the same time,
mutual obedience,
real obedience,
holy listening
forever seeks the spiritual dialogue
holy wisdom demands.

In a Monastery of the Heart,
it is the acceptance of wisdom not our own
that asks of us the spiritual maturity
that listens first and always to the Word of God—
and allows the Word to be the testing ground
of every other demand made on our lives.

It is obedience to the greater law of love.

An authentic claim to obedience
does not deny another person's independence
and autonomy of thought.
On the contrary,
it hones the seeker for the sake
of the growth of the community
and the spreading of the Word.

———

This listening with the heart
to the insights of another
is not the obedience of children,
or soldiers,
or servants,
or minions.
It is the obedience given to a lover,
because of love alone.

19

Conversion of Heart

"It is high time for us to arise from sleep."

Every life is one long list
of defining moments:

At one moment,
we discover that what we have done
with our lives to this point
is not really what we are meant to do.

At another moment,
we come to realize
that we have actually done
very little with our lives at all.

At a different moment,
we plot a course
whose purpose is a better future—

and we struggle with the thought
of the energy
it will take to do it.

At some moment,
we suddenly recognize the fact
that we have been
feverishly expending energy—
like walkers on a treadmill—
going nowhere at all.

Or, just as bad, we become aware
that we have been living
good lives
morally, mentally, materially,
but that in the center of ourselves,
in the heart of our small worlds,
we can see nothing of value,
nothing lasting
to show for it.

We are alive, but only somewhat.
We are good, but only vacantly, at best.
We have kept all the rules,
done all the right things,
said all the right prayers,
but something we cannot even name,
let alone define,
is missing.

We find ourselves
living in a spiritual shell
that runs on routine,
rather than the electricity
of the Spirit.

We are, yes—
we breathe and move and seem to do—
but we are not the cauldron
of purpose and purity of heart
we had always hoped to be.

But Benedictine spirituality reverses that.

To live in the spirit of a Monastery of the Heart
is to be led daily,
from one moment of prayer to the next,
to the depth
of the sacramental life,
to the consciousness
that all of life is sacred
and that every act of ours
makes life either
more—or less—holy.

Benedictine spirituality calls us to the tasks of living
and refuses to allow anything we do
to be lost to the economy

of holiness:
not kitchen tasks,
not reading,
not personal relationships,
not work,
not even our small service to strangers.

It confronts us with a moral determination
to care for the poorest of the poor,
to respect the whole of society,
to open our arms
to the entire gamut of life
and see it as our obligation
to participate in the co-creation
of the world.

It steeps us
in the mind of God,
hour after hour,
day after day,
year after year,
all the days of our lives.

To be a monastic of the heart
prods us to see ourselves—
what we think about,
what we talk about,
what we promote,
what we ignore—

as part of the character
of the world,
not as a bystander,
not as an observer.

It creates in us the awareness
that everything we do
is part of Benedictine asceticism,
everyone we touch
is essential to our building up
of the human community,
every hour we spend
is an anthem, an alleluia,
to the work of God in us.

There is simply nothing that is
unimportant
in Benedictine spirituality.
It is to that sense of wholeness
that Benedictine sanctity aspires.
It is out of that sense of oneness
that Benedictine spirituality
welcomes every person at the door,
takes on every task to be done,
listens to every voice and idea,
inhales every moment of beauty
that sweeps away
all the dross of our souls.

———

Benedictine spirituality
is God-with-us everywhere
at every moment.

It is the integration
of all the little parts of our small lives
into the one great enterprise
of seeking God—
who is at the heart,
in the foundation,
the beginning and the end
of it all—
that is the essence of conversion of heart
in a Benedictine life.

To the Benedictine,
conversion of heart is the turning
of the soul
toward its endpoint
at all times.

Conversion of heart regards nothing as "secular"
or unimportant;
it leaves nothing
out of the equation
of sanctity.

It lives in a state
of continual contemplation,

where the face of God
is as clear as lightning
in the dark—
because we have finally learned
to see beyond everything that is
to the mind of the God
who made it.

The conversion of life
that is at the basis
of Benedictine holiness
comes when,
as a Monastery of the Heart,
we finally realize
that God's will for us
is that we come to realize
that all things are of God—
all the moments of our lives,
however stumbling they may be—
and that all things call us to melt into
one great paean of praise
for the joy of having found
the God we continue to seek.

20

Stability of Heart

"Do not . . . run away from the road that leads to salvation."

The will of God in life
does not come in straight lines,
or clear signs,
or certain choices.

Life is not a set of constants
to which we cling for security
or seek for affirmation.
On the contrary,
life is often confusing
and blurred,
unsure under foot,
tentative and shaky to the touch.

Our relationships do not feel
as firmly fixed as they once did.

The work is no longer invulnerable
to change.
The world around us has tilted and tipped
without our permission.

Nothing is what it once had been,
nothing is what it promised to be.

But one thing is inescapable:
the way we deal with
whatever happens to us
on the outside
will depend entirely
on what we have become
on the inside.

Wherever we have fixed our hearts,
whatever it is to which we have given them,
will determine the way we experience
all that is happening to us now.
Indeed, it is stability of heart,
not stability of place,
that is the real monastic gift.

Stability of heart—
commitment to the life of the soul,
faithfulness to the community,
perseverance in the search for God—
is the mooring

that holds us fast
when the night of the soul
is at its deepest dark,
and the noontime sun sears
the spirit.

When life seems unclear,
out of control,
wavering,
it is stability
in a Monastery of the Heart
that leads us from one day
to the next.

When life tastes least satisfying,
it is stability of heart
that continues to trust
in the zest for life.

When life seems to have abandoned us,
broken its promises,
petered out to nothingness,
it is stability of heart that reminds us
that we are on our way yet
to what we are meant to be—
if we will only stay the course.

"Monastics may be assigned
a burdensome task,"

the ancient Rule teaches.
"If so, they should,
with complete gentleness and obedience,
accept the order given."

Let us continue to trust
that whatever the obstacles we face,
whatever the walls that entrap us,
whatever the spiritual fatigue
that weighs us down,
the God of our heart
is in the midst of it,
waiting for us still
to make it clear.

But stability of heart
in a monastery without walls,
a monastery where single-mindedness
and a common spirit
are the foundation on which we stand,
is not easy.

It is not simple in its meaning
or comfortable in its demands.

Yet it is the promise of stability
that tells us to push on
when we are tired of pushing.

———

Stability of heart tells us that the prayer
and the work
and the service
and the study
and the reading
and the believing
are worth it,
even when all of it
has never felt more useless,
more pointless,
more empty of the God
we had hoped to find there.

Stability is not in vogue
in a world
obsessed with change.

This world tells us to move on
when things get hard.

This world tells us to start over
rather than to finish what we have begun.

The culture of change tells us
to fashion our worlds
according to us,
to refuse the struggles
that come our way,
to hew an easier path

than one according to the Gospels
that lead us beyond
the struggles of the day
to the resurrection of spirit that comes
in their aftermath.

The wisdom of the Rule tells us instead,
"Do not be daunted
immediately by fear
and run away from the road
that leads to salvation.
It is bound to be narrow at the outset."

It is a long journey,
this search for God.
It is constructed of patience and trust,
of perseverance and persistence,
of the routines of dailiness,
and the cataclysmic interruptions of time.

But through it all,
Benedictine spirituality tells us,
there is only one invariant
on which we must depend:
the steadiness—the stability—of the heart of God
and the constancy of knowing that
"as we progress in this way of life
and in faith,"
the Rule assures us,

"we shall run on the path
of God's commandments,
our hearts overflowing
with the inexpressible delight of love."

OUR SPIRITUAL
GROWTH

21

Humility

*"After ascending all these steps of humility, we will quickly arrive
at the 'perfect love' of God which 'casts out fear.'"*

In Benedictine spirituality,
there is a twelve-runged ladder
that leads to God.

This ladder that reaches
between us and God
is called "the steps of humility."

The interesting thing about humility
is that in the Rule—
a document on spiritual development—
its cornerstone principle requires
the acceptance of our earthiness,
the embrace of our humanity
as the very stuff of our holiness.

Our humanity, the Rule implies,
is the clay upon which
the Divine Potter
and the heat of life's kiln
work to shape and glaze
our pliant selves
into vessels of the God-life within.

Humility
is the antidote to the myth
of perfectionism
that eats away at the heart
of the spiritual life,
drowning it in depression,
sinking it in despair,
leading us to abandon
the very thought of a truly
spiritual life—
given the human propensity
to become enmeshed in the very failures
we fear.

It is, as well, an antidote
to an achievement-driven, image-ridden,
competitive society
that is the hallmark of the modern age.

And yet, it is precisely who we are—
with all our moral weaknesses,

all our spiritual fatigue—
that is the stuff of our eventual glory.

The willingness to struggle
with our weaknesses is, in fact,
the very proof of the sincerity
of our commitment
to live life in a Monastery of the Heart.

It is here, in a community of seekers,
sustained by their support
and guided by their wisdom,
that we strive ever more and more
to become the fullness of ourselves
fulfilled in the heart of God.

If this support and guidance
are the very evidence of God's goodness to us,
our ascent up the ladder of humility
is the measure of our response,
because it is here
that we become
most human.

Benedict's ladder of humility begins, oddly,
in surrender to an awareness of
the presence of the God we seek
as already within us,
and it ends in personal serenity.

It links, without apology, both the spiritual
and the material dimensions of life
and makes them one.

It shows us just how tightly woven
our spiritual life—
and the way we live it—
are meant to be.

The function of the spiritual life
is not to reject our humanity
but to acknowledge our neediness
to bring it to fullness.

The steps on the ladder of humility
are clear ones:

The first step of humility
is that we "keep 'the reverence of God
always before our eyes'
and never forget it."

To realize the presence of God—
whatever our own moral state—
makes the spiritual life
a companionship with God,
not God a trophy to be won
by perfect adherence

to all the rules of life—
of which we are obviously perfectly incapable.

The first step of humility dispels
all notions of "merit theology."
We simply do not need to "earn" God—
in fact, we cannot earn God,
none of us,
not even the holiest among us.

The truth is, Benedict teaches,
we already *have* God
and we must not forget it.
We must simply recognize
that God is God—
and we are not.
We are not in control;
we are simply on the way
to recognizing God,
wherever God
may be found.

Humility tells us that God is with us
and within us
always.

The second step of humility
is "that we love not our own will . . .
rather we shall imitate by our actions

that saying of Jesus,
'I have come not to do my own will,
but the will of the One who sent me.'"

The second step of humility
calls us to realize that God's will
is best for us,
whether we understand that will
when we are faced with it or not.

Humility teaches us that the God who is good
wishes me well and not woe,
that I am the dust
God has destined for the stars.
The second step of humility
says that the marrow of the spiritual life
lies in learning to trust the God
who created us.

The third step of humility
is that, for the sake of our growth,
we be willing to put ourselves
under the spiritual guidance
of others—
not to be chained for their use,
not to obey for the sake of "obeying,"
but for the sake of being led
to the very height of our own potential,

beyond our own present insights.

The third step of humility
instills in us that we must be willing
to receive spiritual direction.

The fourth step of humility
is that if "difficult, unfavorable,
or even unjust conditions"
are our lot in life,
that we "endure it without weakening
or seeking escape,"
that we must learn to persevere
in order to discover what darkness—
as well as light—
has to teach us.

Life is not a straight line,
not even the spiritual life.
There are obstacles and obstructions,
resistance and regrets,
in the path everywhere.

Humility enables us to understand
that there are reasons for darkness,
blessings in difficulties,
hope to be gained from struggles
that scour the soul of the dross
of spiritual ennui.

The fourth step of humility
tells us to endure through the mist of life's spiritual night
until the light rises once again in us.

The fifth step of humility,
the Rule says,
is when we "do not conceal . . . any sinful thoughts"
nor "any wrongs committed in secret."
This step of humility
is the unmasking project
of our lives.
It frees us to be who we are
and become who we must,
despite the judgements of others.

It means that we must never allow
our image—even our own image of ourselves,
let alone the image of us held by those around us—
to exceed the real truth about ourselves.

Once we have acknowledged who we are,
there is no amount of calumny that can ever
really hurt us again.

The fifth step of humility says
that acknowledging our faults
will save us from falling victim
to the false impressions

that keep us in public chains
to the ideas of others about us,
that trap us
into pretending to be
who we are not.

The sixth step of humility
counsels us to be
"content with the lowest
and most menial treatment."

In this step of humility
we foreswear the best theater tickets
and car,
the best house and clothes,
the best table at the restaurant,
and the best office in the building.

It means that we don't expect
to be served.
We don't expect to be made
an exception.
We don't expect to be preferred.

It is a freeing experience,
the attainment of this step of humility.

The sixth step of humility says
that when we are satisfied

with whatever we get,
we can never be disappointed again.

The seventh step of humility
is that "we not only admit with our tongues
but are also convinced in our hearts
that we are inferior to all and of less value."

It is at this step on the ladder of humility
that we stop judging others,
that we can really begin to hear
the caring and insightful criticism of others,
because we have finally
admitted to ourselves
both our highest potential
and our greatest weaknesses.

Once we ourselves recognize
to what depths we are capable of sliding,
we stop defending ourselves
from other people's criticisms of us,
from others' questions about us,
and we stop blaming everybody else
for what *we* have surely done.

Gone is the defensiveness
that has cemented us
in an unwillingness to change.

———

We know ourselves now—
human in every dimension,
every desire,
every reaction,
every response—
to be capable of anything
and everything.

More empty now of self,
we no longer react with shock
at the iniquity of another
and begin to empathize instead
with the fissures of soul
with which they also struggle.

We are no longer shocked
or repulsed by the failings we see around us,
because we truly know
that in the same circumstances
we could have, would have,
done the same—or worse—ourselves.

We know who we are—
and who we might have been.
We are no longer so implacably certain
of our own deep-down virtue.

Humility here means
that we have come

to the point where we can
let go of self-righteousness,
knowing that
"There but for the grace of God
go I."

The eighth step of humility
is that "we do only what is endorsed
by the common rule
of the monastery."

To learn from a community
does not mean that every generation does precisely
what every generation before it has done,
that nothing can change
as time goes by,
that holiness lies in the past.

But it *does* mean that the constants
of monastic life
are not monastic practices
but monastic *values*.

How commitment to prayer
was practiced in the sixth century
is merely history.
That commitment to prayer
is regular, psalmic, and scriptural—
and continues even now—

is truly Benedictine.

Peace and care for creation,
concern for human community and work,
discernment, prayer, and prayerful reading,
equality, hospitality, and conversion of heart—
these are eternal Benedictine values.

These are the ideals
upon which the Benedictine tradition rests.

Not to learn these,
not to live these,
is not to be a monastic of the heart.

The eighth step of humility requires us
to take our responsibility
to renew the tradition
in fresh new ways in every age.

The ninth step of humility
is that we "control our tongues
and remain silent,
not speaking unless asked a question."
Learning to listen to the other
is every bit as much a part of humility
as learning to be silent ourselves.

There is such a thing
as a bitter silence,

a barren silence,
a busy silence
that simply cuts
the rest of the world
out of our lives.

But valuing the words of others,
listening to their concerns,
learning from their insights,
admitting their intelligence,
honoring their ideas,
is the very center of human community.

These are the deepest elements
in the human dialogue.
Without them, no dialogue is possible,
only empty, posturing, aimless words.

This ninth step of humility calls us
to listen to everyone around us,
to make no exceptions,
and we will hear the voice of God
in the world.

The tenth step of humility
is that "we are not given to ready laughter,
for it is written,
'Only fools raise their voices in laughter.'"

———

Here the warning is
not against enjoying ourselves,
not against having fun.
It is against making fun and joy
impossible for everybody else.

The warning is directed at
the loud and boisterous
who take all the air out of the room,
who make real conversation impossible,
who draw all attention to themselves,
who lack gravity and reflection
and make it impossible for everyone else, as well.

Here humility leads us
to learn what a really good time is
for everyone else,
and never to use ridicule of another
as the counterfeit of it.

The eleventh step of humility
is that "we speak gently and without laughter . . . ,
briefly and reasonably."

Humility requires that our conversations
are never barbed or bitter,
that we use no group, no community,
for the sake only
of the personal agendas of the self.

———

Benedictine spirituality leads us
to free ourselves
from recrimination
and the acid of revenge.

The eleventh step of humility says that
to be Benedictine,
we must speak words of peace
peacefully,
and words of care
carefully,
and words of love
lovingly,
and all words gently.

Finally,
the twelfth step of humility teaches
"that we always manifest humility
in our bearing no less than in our hearts."

The humble person is not haughty;
does not strut;
does not shout or bully or command
or impose.

The humble person is simple
and quiet
and serene

walking and sitting,
standing and talking,
"or anywhere else . . . ,"
always aware of their own guilt
and so judging no one else's.

It is, in essence, in humility—
in the sense of our place
in the universe—
that the spiritual life
must both begin and end.

Humility speaks of our relationship to God,
our relationship to the spiritual teachers around us,
to the development of the self
beyond self-centeredness,
and finally to what it means to cultivate
humble relationships with others.

Humility teaches us,
ultimately,
that personal growth is a process,
not an event,
and that self-love,
the narcissism that makes us
the center of our own universe,
is destructive
of the self.

———

In the end, the twelve steps are simple ones.
Humility leads us:
1. To recognize that God is God.
2. To know that God's will is best for us.
3. To be willing to receive direction.
4. To endure and don't grow weary.
5. To acknowledge faults.
6. To be content with less than the best.
7. To let go of image making.
8. To learn from the community.
9. To listen to others.
10. To abandon the urge to ridicule.
11. To speak kindly.
12. To be simple; to be serene.

Then Benedict makes the only promise
in the entire Rule:
"After ascending all these steps of humility,
we will quickly arrive
at the 'perfect love' of God
which 'casts out fear.'"

And that is a guarantee
deeply
to be desired.

22

Spiritual Tools

"These are the tools of the spiritual craft."

Benedictine spirituality is clear:
Beware the spirituality,
the Rule implies,
that lacks balance,
that lacks the fullness
of the spiritual life,
that revolves around mystique
and mystery,
around esoteric ritual
or secret knowledge.

Life with God
at its center,
as the beat of its heart,
is far simpler than that.

———

"First of all, 'Love God with your whole heart,
your whole soul
and all your strength,
and love your neighbor
as yourself,'"
Benedict says.

That is the end, the purpose, and the essence
of Benedictine spirituality.
Everything else is practice.

In a Monastery of the Heart
that seeks to make Benedictine spirituality
a living, vibrant part of
contemporary society,
life with God rests in
steeping ourselves in the spiritual traditions
that show us the fundamental path
to love of God
and love of humankind.

Benedict's "Tools for Good Works"
lay out a way of life that is simple and clear,
deeply traditional
yet fully contemporary.

It rests in our becoming fully adult—
in charge of our emotions
and our appetites

and our egotism:
"You are not to act in anger . . . ," the Rule says.
"Rid your heart of all deceit.
Never give a hollow greeting of peace
or turn away when someone
needs your love."

Life with God, it is clear
in the teachings of Benedict,
rests as much on our being
humanly loving members
of the human community
as it does on
regular repetition
of revered religious exercises.

The Tools are a directory
of the cornerstone documents
of the spiritual life—
the commandments,
the corporal
and the spiritual works of mercy,
the steps of humility,
the demands of community,
the dictates of the spiritual life.

They show us what it takes
to develop a holy heart,
to be an involved human being,

a good community member,
a mature person,
a spiritual adult,
a God-centered seeker.

"Your way of acting
should be different
from the world's way,"
Benedict directs.
"The love of God
must come before all else."

Then everything else in life
takes its proper place.

It is these spiritual tools
that call us to come
to the fullness of life
by coming to balance
in all things.

To construct a Monastery of the Heart, then,
is to avoid the kind of extremes
that mask as asceticism,
that play at holiness,
but which, down deep,
work to skew either
our perspective on life
or our appreciation of it.

We must not, in anything,
the Tools remind us,
be given to excesses
that drain us
of the energy for life
or mire us in the kind of disinterest
that distances us
from the demands of life around us.

Spiritual maturity,
we come to see,
requires us to be ardent
in our search for
emotional maturity—
to damp down our petty little jealousies
or our instinct to incite strife,
to love both the young
and the old,
to pray for our enemies
and make peace
before the setting of the sun.

The Tools for Good Works are a call to us
to respect tradition
and, at the same time,
to regard the present
as the place where God
waits for us to grow and create

and become
the best we can be
in our own time.

The Tools demand of us
fidelity to the spiritual practices
that immerse us in the presence of God.
They require us to commit ourselves
to peace and justice,
to the poor and needy,
to honesty and integrity.

And, the Rule reminds us,
even if we have tried and failed in all these things,
tried and failed again,
and tried and failed again,
we must "never lose hope in God's mercy."

Benedictine spirituality
is the strikingly powerful
"middle way"
between indifference to the spiritual life
and extremism in the spiritual life.

Benedict's Tools for Good Works
call us to be monastics of the heart
in whom the commandments
guide our relationship both with God
and with the world in which we live.

With their emphasis on the spiritual
and corporal works of mercy,
they call us, too, to be God-like members
of the human community.
"You must relieve the lot of the poor,"
the Rule teaches,
"'clothe the naked, visit the sick,'
bury the dead,
help the troubled
and console the sorrowing."

They remind us that to be wholly spiritual
we must be wholly human.
We must be humanity at its best,
we must be a fully human human being,
psychologically,
spiritually,
and emotionally mature—
a human being reaching for
the stars that bring us home
to the One
who made us more
than the clay we've been given
to shape on our way.

23

Sacred Art

"They are to practice their craft with all humility."

The bond between Benedictine spirituality and art
goes deep.
Medieval monasteries were centers of the arts
and patrons of the arts
because art, as a reflection of beauty—
which is itself an attribute of God—
came to be understood,
in theological terms,
as simply another sign
of the living presence of God.

Sacred images, music, and architecture
transcend the distractions of matter.
Art gives both consciousness
and expression
to the presence of God in time.

———

Art, monastics of every century knew,
gives us new ways
to see the unseeable.

Soaring spires, awesome cloisters,
and grand chapterhouses
became hallmarks
in ages past of monastic life.

In our own age,
paintings and illuminations,
grand music and great poetry,
deep and honest writing,
and the sculpting of the spiritual
in human form
all speak of the mystical dimensions
of monastic life,
still come out of spirits thirsty for God.

The beauty of creation, of God,
monastics reasoned,
is of the essence of life.
There is a responsibility to nurture it.

No wonder that artists of all ilk
flocked to monasteries across Europe,
to make visible
the infinite dimensions

of the invisible God
and work there yet in its pursuit.

Clearly, the artist and the monastic
seek the same thing.

They are embarked on the same journey.
They are devoted to the same end.
They both believe
that spirit is greater than matter,
but that matter is its borning place.

Monasteries and monastic churches
have always drawn artists
like magnets attract steel.

A Monastery of the Heart, then,
cannot leave the world
or any place in it called Benedictine—
our homes, our work places,
our prayer and reflection areas—
to the deterioration and disorder
that comes from the soul
unattuned to the beauty of God
reflected in the beauty of creation.

Monasticism exists in pursuit of the beauty
of the invisible God.
Art makes shining slivers

of that beauty
visible.
To develop the soul
is to develop the essence of an artist.

Monasticism is the one path of life
that declares itself to be
the single-minded search for God in life—
before which all other pursuits pale.

It is an exercise in living every day
on a plane above itself,
of seeing in the obvious
more than the obvious,
in finding even in the mundane
the creative energy
that drives human creation to heights
that end in bursts of beauty
in the self and in the world around it.

If, indeed, truth is beauty and beauty truth,
then the monastic and the artist are one.

Basic to monasticism
are the very qualities
art demands of the artist:
silence and contemplation,
discernment of spirit and humility.

———

Basic to art are the very qualities
demanded of the monastic:
single-mindedness, the search for beauty,
immersion in praise and creativity.

The meaning of one for the other
makes for both great art
and greatness of soul.

It is a love for human community
that puts the eye of the artist
in the service of truth.
Knowing the spiritual squalor
to which the pursuit of anything less than beauty
can lead us,
the artist lives
to stretch our senses
beyond the tendency
to settle for lesser things—
simplistic stories instead of great literature,
bland characters rather than great portraits,
tasteless decorations instead of artistic accessories,
plastic flowerpots instead of pottery.

Finally, it is humility
that enables an artist
to risk rejection and failure,
disdain and derogation,
to bring to the heart of the world

what the world too easily, too randomly,
too callously
overlooks.

In Benedictine spirituality,
we are all formed in the monastic art
of the search of ultimate Beauty.

Clearly, great art
is a very spiritual thing.
More, a great spiritual life
is itself a piece of great art.
It is the ultimate creativity.

It is an external sign of the interior artistry
of a Monastery of the Heart
to create such beauty,
and then to give its beauty away
as freely and as recklessly
as possible,
so that every human soul
can see in it
another, a better, image of God.

It is one of the great gifts of Benedictine spirituality
that a Monastery of the Heart can give:
that we spend ourselves
making the world as beautiful
as God, the Artist, the Word, meant it to be.

24

Good Zeal

*"Just as there is a wicked zeal of bitterness which separates from
God, so there is a good zeal which leads to God."*

The Rule of Benedict was written
in the sixth century,
in an ascetical climate
more given to personal self-denial
than to the discipline of community building.

If there is any segment
of this Rule, however,
that speaks to its humanity,
its soul,
its basic approach to the spiritual life,
it is the chapter on "The Good Zeal of Monastics."

Rather than calling for strict adherence
to personal disciplines,

the chapter makes an important distinction
between "evil zeal" and "good zeal."

It is an important spiritual reflection
for all of us who set out
to live in a Monastery of the Heart,
where most efforts at the spiritual life
are private and personal,
unmonitored and undefined,
and so always subject
to being either too extreme a reaction
or too little a response.

If there is a temptation
in the spiritual life,
it is, as the Rule makes clear,
"to aspire to be called holy
before you really are."

It is the temptation
to measure ourselves—
and others—
according to the norms
laid down by a distorted zeal,
a neurotic religiosity
that gets satisfaction out of extremes
and calls them "the spiritual life."

Distorted zeal rests for its confirmation

on a series of private exercises designed to test
the spiritual athleticism
of the human spirit.

It calls for rigorous adherence
to personal practices
designed to wear down the body
in order to damp the impulses
of the soul.

Spiritual practices of this sort
call for harsh fasts
and long prayer periods,
for intense regimes of self-denial
and withdrawal,
all of which are sincere, certainly,
all of which are signs of commitment
to the spiritual life.

But at the same time,
all of these practices can be mistaken for
the very thing they seek:
the conversion of heart
that attunes a person
to the will of God
for the world.

Worse, those who practice
this kind of distorted zeal,

make themselves the measure
by which they evaluate
and determine the spiritual life
of others, as well.

Drained of mercy
and sapped of spirit,
they lose contact with
the very God of love
for whom, they say, they search.

The criteria for the good zeal
which the Rule of Benedict
makes the standard
of Benedictine spirituality,
on the other hand,
is that it must be practiced
"with fervent love."

The qualities of good zeal,
as the ancient Rule describes them,
are almost too simple
for souls more interested in
keeping spiritual score
than in living a spiritual life:

We must be zealously devoted
to one another—
in such a way that we give preference

to the needs and wishes
of the other.

We must bear with zealous patience
the infirmities,
"whether of body or mind,"
of those around us.

We must zealously compete with one another
only in our attempt
to listen well
to the wisdom and needs of others,
rather than to center
only on our own.

We must zealously do what is best
for others,
rather than concentrate
simply on what we have decided
is best for ourselves.

We must zealously love one another
chastely and appropriately,
not selfishly
or exploitatively.

We must be in zealous awe
of the presence of God
in us and around us.

We must zealously love our community,
its tradition and its teachers,
with real affection.

Most of all, we must prefer nothing
in the world
to the love of God.

Then, if we do these things—
if we live life
in our Monastery of the Heart—
with this kind of zeal,
we will have reached
the heights of love
to which Benedictine spirituality
is designed to bring us.

25

Peace

"Turn away from evil and do good; let peace be your
quest and aim."

Over the archway
of medieval monasteries
were commonly carved the words
Pax Intrantibus,
"Peace to those who enter here."

These words were both a hope
and a promise.

Benedict's vision
of the peaceable kingdom
was a real one.
In a society
struggling with social chaos,
awash in the evils of classism,

prey to foreign encroachment on all sides,
and at the mercy of wave after wave
of warring forces, highway piracy,
and the wide-spread social disorganization
and moral deterioration
that came with the fall
of the superpower Rome,
Benedict sketched out a blueprint
for world peace.

He laid a foundation
for a new way of life,
the ripples of which stretched
far beyond the first monastery gates
to every culture and continent,
from one generation to another,
from that era to this one,
from his time
and now to ours.
To us.

Peace is our legacy, our mandate,
our mission,
as alive today as ever,
more in need today—
in a nuclear world,
a world of starving peoples—
than ever.

———

Benedictine peace, however,
is not simply
the absence of war.
It is a lifestyle
that makes war unacceptable
and violence unnecessary.

It is not a lifestyle dominated by control
and a plethora of rules.
It is a lifestyle
that foregoes violence
on every level,
for any reason.

Most of all, this lifestyle is a simple one.
It is basic in its elements,
not difficult to achieve,
simple to sustain.
It nurtures neither
ambition nor greed.

It is straightforward in its values,
without being either esoteric
or convoluted.

These values are clear ones:
community,
prayer,
stewardship,

equality,

stability,

conversion,

peace—

all make for communities of love.

It is a lifestyle committed to its ideals

before all else,

and intent on opening its arms

and taking the world

into its Monastery of the Heart.

It is, then, an oasis of human peace

in a striving, searing, simmering world.

Benedictine spirituality is a counterculture

that calls for a rhythm of life

that honors and enables,

stretches and challenges,

every dimension of human development.

It creates community out of a collection of strangers—

a slice of life

that crosses age levels,

economic backgrounds,

and ethnicities—

to where differences

can be honored,

and differences

can be broached,
and peace can come
to both the person
and to an entire population
at the same time.

Benedictine spirituality
is a life that honors the earth
and cultivates the planet
for the sake of all the people
of the earth.
It is a holy life.
It passes on to the next generation
a society and a globe
that is in better condition
than it was—
because people with a Benedictine heart
have taken their responsibility
to protect it for the future.

It allows no waste
but provides for
the needs of all.

It allows no class distinctions
but thrives on the exceptions
that the human condition
demands.

———

It aims for the highest standards
of personal behavior
and, at the same time,
understands and supports those
for whom growth
is a struggle
and the social standards of life
seem always to be a work in progress.

Finally, Benedictine spirituality
requires of us all
the humility
that allows us no room
to make gods of ourselves,
to impose ourselves on the rest
of the universe,
to develop the hubris that leads
to the oppression of others,
that justifies force
as the sign of our superiority,
that enthrones the arrogance in us
over the holiness and wholeness of others,
that smothers the awareness in a person
of their small and proper place
in the universe.

It is humility that makes us happy
with what we have,
willing to have less,

kind to all,
simple in our bearing,
and serene within ourselves.

It teaches us that they who have
themselves for God
have a very small god indeed.

Benedictine spirituality
is a recipe for peace
and a prescription for a life
lived well
on every level.

And now, in our Monastery of the Heart,
it is ours to shape
and to preserve,
to share and to promote,
to model and to make real
in our own time.

Pax Intrantibus.
Peace to those who enter here.

Epilogue

"As we progress in this way of life and in faith, we shall run on the path of God's commandments, our hearts overflowing with the inexpressible delight of love."

Benedictine spirituality
is not a spiritual practice
that waxes and wanes,
comes and goes,
as we grow
and change
and mature in the spiritual life.

It is a way of life,
a free-standing and stable model
of the God-seeking human enterprise
that is based on age-old traditions
and ancient wisdom.

———

Nor is it a goal unto itself.
It is, as the Rule says
so directly and simply,
"written for beginners."

This is the life that introduces us
to a lifestyle,
not to a set of prayer practices
or even any defined ministry.

It is not a work that can be accomplished
in any given period
and then forgotten.
It is the work of a lifetime.

It roots us in the scriptures
and prayer.

It immerses us in the work
of co-creation.

It stresses justice as the way to peace.

It does away with classism,
racism,
sexism,
and ethnocentrism.

It sees differences

as the enrichment of any community,
rather than a threat to society.

It urges us to immersion
in the Word of God,
respect for study and reflection,
and regularity at prayer.

And yet, Benedictine spirituality calls for
"nothing harsh, nothing burdensome."

It leaves to each of us,
as individuals and groups,
the task of determining
in every community,
of every era,
what is necessary
to fulfill
these values
and attain the riches
of this life.

It calls us always to the *more* of life:
to more peace,
more humility,
more serenity,
more study,
more prayer,
more openness,

more service of the other,
more community of heart,
more richness of soul,
more immersion in the tradition
and the wisdom it has handed on to us.

It invites us to come to learn, too,
how less is also more:
how less competition means more peace,
less jealousy means more contentment,
less need for things means more satisfaction,
less self-centeredness means more happiness,
and less corrosive personal ambition
leaves more room
for the loving presence of God.

This is a Rule, a spirituality, a lifestyle
in which up is down,
and low is high,
and nothing is everything.

Welcome to the joys that come to the spirit
the less we plague the soul with things.

Welcome to the real riches that life
has to offer.

To those seekers
who find in their souls

a Monastery of the Heart,
the possibility of happiness is unbounded,
the promise of fulfillment is eternal.

Appendix

Monasteries of the Heart is a movement of seekers interested in becoming part of a community of seekers, either online or with others of their own choosing, who form to support one another in shaping their spiritual lives around Benedictine values and priorities. www.monasteriesoftheheart.org